From the National Best-Selling Author of
Understanding the Dreams You Dream

Understanding the Book of Revelation

BLESSED IS HE WHO READS AND THOSE WHO HEAR
THE WORDS OF THIS PROPHECY

Ira Milligan

ISBN: 979-8-9877359-6-1 (paperback)
ISBN 979-8-9877359-2-3 (hardcover)
ISBN 979-8-9877359-7-8 (digital)
Copyright © 2022 by Ira Milligan

All rights reserved. No part of this publication may be reproduced, distributed, or transmitted in any form or by any means, including photocopying, recording, or other electronic or mechanical methods without the prior written permission of the publisher. For permission requests, solicit the publisher via the address below.

Published by: Servant Ministries Inc.
PO Box 1120
Tioga, LA 71477

For information concerning having a seminar conducted in your church, contact Ira at:
www.servant-ministriesinc.org
PO Box 1120 Tioga, LA. 71477

All references to Greek word definitions are from *Strong's Exhaustive Concordance*, Thomas Nelson Publishers, 1990. Unless otherwise indicated, all Scripture references are taken from the New King James Version. Copyright 1979, 1980, 1982 by Thomas Nelson, Inc. Used by permission. All rights reserved.

Italics are used throughout for clarity of expression and for emphasis. They are used in select portions of scriptural quotations for the same reason.

All proper name definitions are taken from *A Dictionary of Scripture Proper Names*, J. B. Jackson, Copyright 1909.

Printed in the United States of America

This book is dedicated to my mother, Mabel Price, who always encouraged and admonished us to do that which was difficult with her indomitable "where there's a will, there's a way!" And, indeed, she was right.

Contents

Acknowledgment vii
Introduction ix

Chapter 1: Revelation's Structure and Symbolism 1
Chapter 2: Revelation's Introduction 11
Chapter 3: Opening the Seven Seals 15
Chapter 4: The Reformation 29
Chapter 5: The Sixth Seal 39
Chapter 6: Open Heavens 51
Chapter 7: War in Heaven 59
Chapter 8: Rejoicing in Victory 63
Chapter 9: The Lord's Army 71
Chapter 10: Revelation's Time Line 77
Chapter 11: Revelation's Time Line Expanded 87
Chapter 12: The Seven Tribulation Trumpets 119
Chapter 13: The Seven Bowls of Wrath 141
Chapter 14: Jezebel and the Antichrist's Judgment 161
Chapter 15: The Millennial Kingdom 179
Chapter 16: The Great White Throne 187
Chapter 17: The New Jerusalem 195
Chapter 18: The Lamb's Bride 199
Chapter 19: The River of Life 205

Bibliography 211
Suggested Readings 213
Other Titles by Ira Milligan 215

Acknowledgment

I wish to express my heartfelt thanks to those precious saints of God who support us with their prayers and substance to allow us to give ourselves wholly to prayer and to the ministry of the Word. A special thanks goes to my wife, Judy, and my friends for proofreading the manuscript.

Introduction

In today's threatening, swiftly changing climate of world events, there has never been a more important time in all of history to understand the mysteries contained in Revelation. Also, there is no other book in the Bible that promises a special blessing upon those who read and heed its instructions. But herein lies the rub—very few readers understand its structure and symbolism, so very few are able to follow its instructions and heed its warnings! Therefore, I've written this book to help guide those who have long been intrigued and puzzled by John's carefully constructed, prophetic forecast of church and world history.

> Blessed is he who *reads* and those who *hear* the words of this prophecy, and *keep* those things which are written in it; for the time is near. (Rev. 1:3; italics mine)

When the Holy Spirit first instructed me to tackle what I consider the most complex book in the Bible and write a commentary on it, I was hesitant to attempt the assignment. But God is faithful. He never gives you a difficult task to do without also giving you the assurance that He gave Gideon, "Surely I will be with you" (Judg. 6:16). To Christ, and Christ alone, goes *all* the praise and credit for this commentary!

Although I certainly do not claim to understand *all* that John wrote, as the reader will see, much of what he prophesied has already come to pass, and we are now living in the fulfillment of the latter days of most of his prophecy.

Understanding where we are on Revelation's prophetic time line is invaluable. Without it, we are like a person lost in a large city, and although we have a map showing where we need to go, we don't know our present location, so the map is useless to us. Without a street sign or prominent landmark revealing our present location, we don't know which way to proceed. Likewise, knowing where we are in history's time line will help us see what lies ahead. Knowing what to expect is necessary because without it, we won't be expecting or prepared for what lies ahead.

I've written this book in commentary style; therefore, much of it is examined verse by verse, symbol by symbol, although to avoid making it too long and tedious, I've passed over small sections of it that are self-explanatory. I've also added many supportive and confirming biblical references to aid and encourage the readers in their study.

Because history is progressive and there are few "hard breaks" in time to allow precise dating of some of John's prophesied events, some of the dates in this book are approximate rather than definitive. Nevertheless, this book will reveal where we are, what signs and obstacles lie ahead, and what we should prepare for as we journey on toward our eternal destination.

Chapter 1

Revelation's Structure and Symbolism

John tells us that the revelation that God gave him consists of "things which must shortly take place" and that Jesus instructed him to "write the things which you have seen, and the things which are, and the things which will take place after this" (Rev. 1:1, 19). John was one of the first disciples that Jesus called, so he was with Him from the beginning of His ministry, but not before that. Therefore, when interpreting Revelation, it is important to remember that nothing in Revelation is applicable to events that occurred before Christ's earthly ministry began.

> The Revelation of Jesus Christ, which God gave Him to show His servants—things *which must shortly take place*. And He sent and *signified* it by His angel to His servant John. (Rev. 1:1; italics mine)

John said that the angel that communicated the Revelation to him *signified* it, meaning that he showed it to him using symbolic language. To understand Revelation, when possible, one must properly interpret each, individual symbol or the interpretation will be incorrect, and the message that the passage contains will be missed, incomplete, or applied incorrectly.

Revelation consists of a visitation from Christ and three partially overlapping visions that the apostle John experienced while he was in exile on the island of Patmos, "for the word of God and the testimony of Jesus Christ" (see Revelation 1:9). Each vision begins with an invitation for him to "come and see" something from a heavenly perspective.

Each vision starts at a distinct point in time and ends at a specific event in history. Within each vision, many things are shown to him more than once, but from different viewpoints. Because of this, certain events appear to occur more than once, but they are simply the same things being seen from different perspectives. Identifying these often repeated and overlapping events enables us to place them on their proper historical time line, even though some are yet in the future, such as the rapture of the church and the outpouring of God's fiery wrath upon the ungodly.

John's three visions, and many of the things contained within his visions, with few exceptions, are *not* chronological. The only way we can develop an actual chronological time line and see the order in which they unfold is to rearrange the various events to coincide with one another. Therefore, to make Revelation understandable, I have rearranged the events in the order that they have already occurred or will occur in the future. In the case of future events, they are placed in the order that they will transpire as they are fulfilled.

John begins by explaining where he was when Jesus appeared to him and gave him specific instructions to write Revelation. During this visit, Jesus dictates seven letters to seven churches in Asia, and John is told to deliver them to the messengers of those churches. Then he is caught up into his first vision:

> After these things I looked, and behold, a door standing open in heaven. And the first voice which I heard was like a trumpet speaking with me, saying, "Come up here, and I will show you

things which must take place after this." (Rev. 4:1)

John's first vision, which is the longest of the three, begins with him being shown a seven-sealed scroll and concludes with him seeing the final outpouring of God's wrath upon the ungodly (Rev. 4:1–16:21). In his second vision, an angel shows him the "judgment of the great harlot who sits on many waters" and concludes with him being shown a "new heaven and a new earth" (Rev. 17:1–21:8).

John's last and shortest vision begins in Revelation 21:9, where he is shown "the great city, the holy Jerusalem, descending out of heaven" and concludes with an invitation for everyone who thirsts to come and drink of the waters of life. This invitation is followed by a warning for the reader to neither add to nor take away anything from what he has written (Rev. 21:9–22:20).

John's three visions are like a jigsaw puzzle, with many interlocking pieces. To show the full, glorious picture of Christ they reveal, I have assembled the scattered pieces chronologically by properly overlaying the various events one upon the other. Then many scriptures found in the other prophetic books are inserted to make the picture clear. Once assembled, a wonderful, beautiful motion picture comes into focus—Jesus the Christ is revealed as the glorious, conquering King who rules over all kings and kingdoms of the world!

The letters to the seven churches found in Revelation chapters 2 and 3 are actually prophecies concerning seven successive church ages. The first of these ages was already in existence when John wrote the letters. For those who question whether the letters are actually prophetic messages forecasting the condition of the church in ages to come—versus being personal letters written to seven individual churches—note that each letter says, "Hear what the Spirit says to the *churches.*" In the day that John wrote Revelation, there was only one church in each city. Therefore, if each letter was meant only for the city and church it was addressed to, it would have said, "Hear what the Spirit says to the *church,*" not "to the *churches.*"

We will see that the seven letters give us the history of the ages, and the seals are opened in response to the condition of the church and the world toward the end of each age. Once a particular church age is birthed, it continues until the end, so the lessons learned and warnings given apply to all the churches from that time forward. All seven churches exist at this present time. Therefore, both the commendations and the corrections that Christ gave to them then apply to all of us now.

In Revelation, John places the seven letters to the churches before the introduction of a scroll that is sealed with seven seals. In reality, the gospel was first introduced to the world when the scroll's first seal was opened, which took place on the day of Pentecost. Accordingly, as stated above, I have placed each seal, with its corresponding letter (or letters), in its proper chronological order.

Another important point to consider is the things that John saw, such as the seals or church ages, usually open or commence at a specific point in time (usually associated with a specific event, as when Martin Luther initiated the Protestant reformation when he nailed the ninety-five theses to the door of Wittenberg's Castle Church in 1517). But it often takes decades or sometimes even centuries for the prophecies concerning these events to completely unfold.

Also, the things that John saw in heaven have their counterpart here on earth. We can be confident that Jesus' prayers will be answered. He prayed, "Your kingdom come. Your will be done on earth as it is in heaven" (Matt. 6:10). Therefore, as time unfolds, we can expect to see both the kingdom and the Father's will fully manifested here on earth. For example, John's first vision begins with an invitation for him to ascend into the throne room of heaven:

> After these things I looked, and behold, a door standing open in heaven. And the first voice which I heard was like a trumpet speaking with me, saying, "Come up here, and I will show you things which must take place after this." Immediately I was in the Spirit; and behold, a throne set in heaven, and One sat on the throne. And He who sat there was like a jasper and a sardius stone in appearance; and there was a rain-

bow around the throne, in appearance like an emerald. (Rev. 4:1–3)

John describes Jesus as appearing like a jasper and a sardius stone, with a rainbow appearing like an emerald around the throne. Jasper means "he will be made prominent" and sardius means "ruddiness" (see 1 Samuel 16:12). A rainbow signifies God's covenant with His people and an emerald, which means *enameled* (i.e., covered) is a beautiful green (signifying *life*). Thus the One on the throne (Jesus) is made prominent (as King David was), and He is the embodiment of God's beautiful covenant of eternal life that all His saints are called to partake of and enjoy (see John 11:25).

Likewise, the four living creatures that John saw around the throne are symbolic of Christ's faithful, anointed, and ordained ministers:

> Before the throne there was a sea of glass, like crystal. And in the midst of the throne, and around the throne, were four living creatures full of eyes in front and in back. The first living creature was like a lion, the second living creature like a calf, the third living creature had a face like a man, and the fourth living creature was like a flying eagle. The four living creatures, each having six wings, were full of eyes around and within. And they do not rest day or night, saying: "Holy, holy, holy, Lord God Almighty, Who was and is and is to come!" (Rev. 4:6–8)

There are *four*, which means *rule* or *dominion*, so these are *ruling* creatures. The first living creature is like a lion, which represents the anointing and ministry of the apostle; the second is like a calf (or young bullock, used to pull the plow), representing the evangelist; the third has a face like a man, representing the pastor-teacher; and the fourth is like an eagle, which represents the office and anointing of the prophet. Also, the creatures "are full of eyes," representing *the eyes of their understanding*—indicating that they are full of *wisdom,* and wings, which represent *spirit* or *anointing*. Therefore, in the order that John saw them, the administration of these four living creatures is manifested here on earth through the ministry of the apostles, evangelists, pastor-teachers, and prophets in the church. They are commissioned to bring glory to God throughout the earth (see Ephesians 1:16–18).

Another symbol that John saw is the twenty-four elders who were seated around the throne. Although there may actually be twenty-four elders who are privileged to always be in Christ's presence and minister to Him in heaven, their manifestation here on the earth is what is important to us. As it often is, the key to interpreting this symbol is found by interpreting the numbers—two means to *divide* (*separate*) or *judge,* and as we saw above, four means to *rule*—so the twenty-four elders who John saw in heaven have their counterpart here on the church as elders who are separated unto God (holy) and who bear rule in the church. So the twenty-four elders in heaven represent all the church's holy, ruling elders who are active here on earth (see 1 Timothy 5:17; Hebrews 13:17).

Another point to consider is this: Christ sits on the throne of David, and David was crowned king two separate times—first over his own brethren, in Hebron, and then over all Israel. Likewise, Jesus is first crowned king over His brethren—those who are adopted into His Father's family and kingdom (the saints, as it is now)—and afterward, over the whole world. The first coronation took place after His resurrection and ascension. The second coronation will take place at the sounding of the seventh trumpet (see Acts 2:36; Revelation 11:15–18).

Paul said that God has "raised us up together, and made us sit together in the heavenly places in Christ Jesus" (Eph. 2:6). As we examine Revelation in detail, we will see that it is paramount for the saints to realize that not only the elders but that we are *all* seated with Christ in heaven's throne room.

Because throughout history various events occur more than once, it should be noted that the things that John prophesied aren't isolated events that only affect a few people, but rather they are events that affect the whole world—things that are worldwide in their manifestation. For example, Paul gave us this warning:

> But know this, that in the last days perilous times will come: For men will be lovers of themselves, lovers of money, boasters, proud, blasphemers, disobedient to parents, unthankful, unholy, unloving, unforgiving, slanderers, without self-control, brutal, despisers of good, traitors, headstrong, haughty, lovers of pleasure rather than lovers of God, having a form of godliness but denying its power. And from such people turn away! (2 Tim. 3:1–5)

The problem is this: There has always been men who are "lovers of themselves," and as long as money has been around, there have been men who love it. Likewise, there has always been men who are boasters, proud, traitors, and the like, but not to the scale that they are when Paul's warning is actually fulfilled. In other words, until the events that are prophesied are worldwide, or they affect the whole earth, it isn't the actual fulfillment that we're looking for.

For example, when the twin towers were destroyed in New York City on September 11, 2001, the resultant fallout has had worldwide implications. It has changed air travel in every nation. Also, it has made all nations aware of the ominous threat of terrorism that exists throughout the world. Therefore, it was and is a sign to the whole world that "perilous times" have come, and since Paul stated that his prophecy would come to pass "in the last days," we can date Paul's prophecy from that date forward.

To understand scriptures such as Revelation 1:1, where John was shown "things which must shortly take place" and statements such as, "Behold I am coming quickly," one must learn to see time from God's perspective. John wrote Revelation around AD 90, and although some of what he saw already existed at the time he wrote, as we will see, most of it unfolded as the centuries passed. Likewise, nearly two thousand years have transpired since Christ said that He was "coming quickly," and He still hasn't arrived. The explanation is this: God, who transcends time—where one day is as a thousand years and a thousand years is as a day—references time by events that are relevant to one another, not by the rotation of the earth. For example, Christ's ascension took place ten days before Pentecost, and the next important event on His agenda, *relevant to His departure*, is His *return*, so He is "coming quickly." The actual number of calendar years is completely irrelevant (see 2 Peter 3:8).

And most important of all, the symbols in Revelation must be interpreted by the Bible itself instead of being based upon someone's personal opinion. The only authority qualified to correctly interpret the Scriptures are the Scriptures themselves. As Peter said,

> And so we have the prophetic word confirmed, which you do well to heed as a light that shines in a dark place, until the day dawns and the *morning star* rises in your hearts; knowing this first, that no prophecy of Scripture is of any private interpretation, for prophecy never came by the will of man, but holy men of God spoke as they were moved by the Holy Spirit. (2 Pet. 1:19–21; italics mine)

Symbols usually have more than one meaning, so one must be careful to search for and apply the correct *biblical* meaning when interpreting them, according to the context they are being used in. For example, a *star* can mean *Christ*, as in the scripture above, or a *saint* or a *minister*, as in Daniel 12:3, "Those who are wise shall shine like the brightness of the firmament, and those who turn many to righteousness like the stars forever and ever." Or a star can represent *Satan*, as in Revelation 9:1, "Then the fifth angel sounded: and I saw a star fallen from heaven to the earth. To him was given the key to the bottomless pit." To always interpret stars as angels, as many saints do, is a misleading error.

Other symbols, such as thunder, which is used on eight different occasions in Revelation, are even more difficult to interpret, unless one makes a careful examination of their usage in other scriptural passages. In the case of thunder, which signifies *change*, it often, but not always, announces a *governmental* change, as when God gave the law to Israel (Exod. 20:18) or when Saul was crowned king (1 Sam. 12:18–19).

A common symbol found throughout Revelation is a beast. A beast usually represents a *king*, including, but not limited to, the Antichrist, or a *kingdom*, which may consist of one or more nations—thus one can have one beast (kingdom) with seven heads (nations), as in Revelation 13:1. Also, a beast can, and often does, represent a powerful, *evil person*, as Hitler and his henchman in Germany were.

Another symbol, similar to beasts, is a horn. Horns usually represent *power and authority*, because the inherent characteristic of most animals with horns is strength or power. So horns often represent *kings*. Solomon said, "Where the word of a king is, there is power; And who may say to him, 'What are you doing?'" (Eccles. 8:4).

And the last thing we need to address before diving into Revelation is translation error. Words in the Greek language, like all languages, often have more than one meaning, or may not have an exact English equivalent.

This is especially true concerning the many precious stones named in Revelation. Although different colors have distinctive meanings, the actual color of many of these stones is uncertain. For example, in nature, jasper may be found in four different color varieties—red, yellow, brown, and green—so the color John saw is unknown. Where possible, I have provided the meaning of the various stones' names, but even the identity of some of the stones has been lost in antiquity, so I cannot always provide a full, definitive explanation of what John meant where precious stones are involved.

Another problem is when a Greek word is assumed to mean one thing when the context requires a different translation. For example, although *angelos* is usually translated "angel," its literal meaning is "messenger." Therefore, instead of the letters to the seven churches being addressed to the *angels* of the churches, *angelos* should be translated as the *messengers* of the churches, which in this case, the messenger is the apostle of the church.

Paul said, "If anyone inquires about Titus, he is my partner and fellow worker concerning you. Or if our brethren are inquired about, they are messengers [Greek: *apostolos*, i.e., apostles] of the churches, the glory of Christ" (2 Cor. 8:23).

Both then and now, it isn't the *angel* of the church that needs to read and apply God's message; it is the one who is responsible to give guidance and correction to the church—the church's *apostle*! But that's the subject of another book!

Chapter 2

Revelation's Introduction

> I was in the Spirit on the Lord's Day, and I heard behind me a loud voice, as of a trumpet…, Then I turned to see the voice that spoke with me. And having turned I saw seven golden lampstands, and in the midst of the seven lampstands One like the Son of Man, clothed with a garment down to the feet and girded about the chest with a golden band. His head and hair were white like wool, as white as snow, and His eyes like a flame of fire; His feet were like fine brass, as if refined in a furnace, and His voice as the sound of many waters; He had in His right hand seven stars, out of His mouth went a sharp two-edged sword, and His countenance was like the sun shining in its strength. (Rev. 1:10, 12–16)

We will examine this passage in detail because many of the symbols introduced here are used throughout Revelation. John said that he was *in the Spirit*, meaning that he was fully conscious of the presence of God. While in that state of spiritual consciousness, he heard a loud voice behind him sounding like a trumpet. The *voice sounding like a trumpet* introduces one of many, important symbols used in Revelation. A trumpet is symbolic of a *loud voice*, as when one preaches or exhorts the people. An example is when God told Isaiah to "Cry aloud, spare not; *Lift up your voice like a trumpet*; Tell My people their transgression, And the house of Jacob their sins" (Isa. 58:1; italics mine).

In Israel, the trumpet was blown for several different reasons, including to call the tribes together for assembly or to warn them to prepare for war. Paul said, "For if the trumpet makes an uncertain sound, who will prepare himself for battle?" (1 Cor. 14:8). It was also blown to announce the beginning of special occasions, such as the seven feasts of Israel, or to consecrate a public fast: "Blow the trumpet in Zion, Consecrate a fast, Call a sacred assembly" (Joel 2:15).

The trumpets found in Revelation are blown to announce or release many different things, such as the seven severe chastisements of the great tribulation or the rapture. Jesus said that when the rapture occurs, God

> will send His angels with *a great sound of a trumpet*, and they will gather together His elect from the four winds, from one end of heaven to the other [and] Do not marvel at this; for the hour is coming in which all who are in the graves will hear His voice [as a great sound of a trumpet] and come forth—those who have done good, to the resurrection of life, and those who have done evil, to the resurrection of condemnation. (Matt. 24:31; John 5:28–29; italics mine)

When Jesus first appeared to John, he turned to hear the voice behind him and saw seven golden lampstands, which Jesus interpreted as seven churches that John was told to write letters to (see Revelation 1:4, 20). Why lampstands? Because the church is raised up to be a light in the darkness, a city set upon a hill. In the midst of the seven lampstands, John saw "One like the Son of Man, clothed with a garment down to the feet and girded about the chest with a golden band." Obviously, the Son of Man is Jesus, and He is clothed with a robe of righteousness. The belt around His chest is made of gold, which is symbolic of *glory*. Since Paul said that our breastplate is righteousness, Jesus is armored with the glorious righteousness of God (see Ephesians 6:14).

Jesus' head and hair were white like wool. Hair is a *covering* and white, although often seen as righteousness, actually means *pure*, as in unmixed or undefiled. Our robes of righteousness are white, because God's gift of righteousness makes us pure and unblameable in His sight. Jesus' eyes were like a flame of fire. In this passage, eyes and fire are similar in meaning—eyes are symbolic of *desire,* and fire symbolizes *passion,* or sometimes *affliction* (besides *desire*, eyes may also symbolize *understanding*, as when Paul prayed for the Ephesians for the *eyes of their understanding* to be enlightened to the mysteries of Christ; see Ephesians 1:16–18).

Christ's passion is to purge the earth of everything that defiles so that things on earth will be as they are in heaven, pure and undefiled. Therefore, in His passion for purity, He afflicts ungodly sinners in hope that they will repent and turn from their wicked ways. This includes, when necessary, afflicting His own brethren!

His feet were like fine, refined brass. Both feet and brass are symbolic of *words*. "The words of the LORD are pure words, like silver [*or brass*] tried [*refined*] in a furnace of earth, purified seven times" (Ps. 12:6; see also Romans 10:14–15).

John said that the voice that he turned to see was *as the sound of many waters*. Water may represent *spirit*, including the Holy Spirit, and *words*, including God's word (Jesus said, "The words that I speak to you are spirit, and they are life" [John 6:63; see also Ephesians 5:26]). Also, waters may represent *people*. So in this case, the *sound of many waters* that John heard represents the prophetic voice of many saints speaking in unison.

Jesus' right hand held seven stars. Stars may symbolize people or angels, but as we shall see later, the most common meaning is people. John saw a sharp, two-edged sword coming out of Christ's mouth, and His countenance was like the sun shining in its strength. Paul tells us that the "sword of the Spirit is the word of God," and one of the psalms says that God is a *sun* (see Ephesians 6:17; Psalm 84:11).

When Jesus appeared to Paul on the road to Damascus, Paul said that he saw a light from heaven that was brighter than the midday sun, shining around him and those who were journeying with him, and they all fell to the ground. In fact, Jesus' countenance was so bright that it blinded Paul! (See Acts 26:12–13.) Jesus' glorious presence also had a profound affect upon John:

> And when I saw Him, I fell at His feet as dead. But He laid His right hand on me, saying to me, "Do not be afraid; I am the First and the Last. The mystery of the seven stars which you saw in My right hand, and the seven golden lampstands: The seven stars are the angels [Greek: *angelos*] of the seven churches, and the seven lampstands which you saw are the seven churches." (Rev. 1:17–20)

Seven means *complete*. Therefore, the seven churches represent *all* the churches, everywhere, and as we observed in the previous chapter, in this context, *angelos* should be translated "messengers" rather than angels.

Chapter 3

Opening the Seven Seals

The Seven-Sealed Scroll

Revelation's story actually begins with those who are both in heaven and on earth lamenting the fact that no one is worthy to open a seven-sealed scroll held in the right hand of the One who sat on the throne.

> And I saw in the right hand of Him who sat on the throne a scroll written inside and on the back, sealed with seven seals. Then I saw a strong angel proclaiming with a loud voice, "*Who is worthy to open the scroll and to loose its seals?*" And no one in heaven or on the earth or under the earth was able to open the scroll, or to look at it. So I wept much, because no one was found worthy to open and read the scroll, or to look at it. (Rev. 5:1–4; italics mine)

The identity of this seven-sealed scroll is really not a mystery at all. Since Scripture always interprets Scripture, the answer is found in the Bible. *This scroll is the book of life.* It corresponds to the tree of life in the garden of Eden that was sealed after Adam sinned (see Genesis

3:24). It is the one book that no one, other than Christ Himself, was worthy to open!

> But one of the elders said to me, "Do not weep. Behold, *the Lion of the tribe of Judah*, the Root of David, has prevailed to open the scroll and to loose its seven seals." And I looked, and behold, in the midst of the throne and of the four living creatures, and in the midst of the elders, stood *a Lamb as though it had been slain*, having seven horns and seven eyes, which are the seven Spirits of God sent out into all the earth. Then He came and took the scroll out of the right hand of Him who sat on the throne. (Rev. 5:5–7; italics mine)

Notice that the *Lion* of the tribe of Judah *prevailed* to open the scroll, but the *Lamb* is the One who actually opens the seals. Why the distinction? The Lion of Judah represents Christ's victorious resurrection from the dead, and the Lamb who was slain from the foundation of the world represents His sacrificial offering, without which we would not be worthy to obtain eternal life (see Revelation 13:8). The following song sung by the four living creatures and twenty-four elders testifies to that fact:

> And they sang a new song, saying: "You are worthy to take the scroll, And to open its seals; For You were slain, And have redeemed us to God by Your blood Out of every tribe and tongue and people and nation, And have made us kings and priests to our God; And we shall reign on the earth." (Rev. 5:9–10)

The Lamb has seven *horns* and seven *eyes*, which represent the seven spirits of God that is sent into the earth. These seven spirits (or *anointings*) are found in Isaiah 11:2–3. Seven means complete, so the seven spirits represent the totality of God's transferable attributes that are available to His ministers:

> The Spirit of the LORD shall rest upon Him, The Spirit of *wisdom* and *understanding*, The Spirit of *counsel* and *might*, The Spirit of *knowledge* and of the *fear of the LORD*. His delight is in the fear of the LORD, And He shall not *judge* by the sight of His eyes, Nor decide by the hearing of His ears. (Italics mine)

John said that the Lamb has made us *kings* and *priests* to our God. Although the priesthood aspect of Christ's ministry has been faithfully experienced by the church for centuries, the kingly aspect has not. Peter said the church is "a holy priesthood, to offer up spiritual sacrifices acceptable to God through Jesus Christ" (1 Pet. 2:5). But we are also spiritual *kings* with *authority over all the power of the enemy* (see Luke 10:19; italics mine). We will discuss this kingly authority to rule over darkness in greater detail later.

Then John saw and heard more than one hundred million angels ministering around the Lamb's throne, saying with a loud voice the sevenfold blessing of the Lamb:

> Then I looked, and I heard the voice of many angels around the throne, the living creatures, and the elders; and *the number of them was ten thousand times ten thousand, and thousands of thousands,* saying with a loud voice: "Worthy is the Lamb who was slain To receive *power* and *riches* and *wisdom*, And *strength* and *honor* and *glory* and *blessing*!" (Rev. 5:11–12; italics mine)

THE WHITE HORSE (AD 30–100)

The first seal was opened fifty days after Christ's resurrection, on the day of Pentecost, which was about AD 30. At this time, He poured out the Holy Spirit upon the 120 believers who tarried in prayer in the upper room in Jerusalem:

> Now I saw when the Lamb opened one of the seals; and I heard one of the four living creatures saying with a voice like thunder, "Come and see." And I looked, and behold, a *white horse*. He who sat on it had a *bow*; and a crown was given to him, and he went out *conquering* and *to conquer*. (Rev. 6:1–2; italics mine)

Although many theologians have taught that the rider of the white horse depicted here is the Antichrist, there is absolutely no scriptural support for that assumption. Why would Jesus release the Antichrist upon the world as His first act upon accepting the crown and assuming the throne? The white horse is the Holy Spirit, and the rider is none other than Christ Himself! The bow in His hand represents the power of the gospel (see 2 Kings 6:22; Romans 1:16). John himself identifies the white horse's rider as Christ:

> Now I saw heaven opened, and behold, a white horse. And He who sat on him was called Faithful and True, and in righteousness He judges and makes war… He was clothed with a robe dipped in blood, and *His name is called The Word of God.* (Rev. 19:11, 13; italics mine)

The resurrected Christ went forth *conquering* through the power of the Holy Spirit, beginning on the day of Pentecost. This is signified by the white horse and its rider. Thus, we can place a definitive date upon the opening of the first seal (AD 30). The first seal foretold of the powerful effectiveness and success that the gospel had in the first century. It also gave a prophetic promise of a second period of conquest in the future. John said the rider went forth "conquering" (beginning in the first century) and "to conquer," thus signifying that he will conquer once again when He rides the white horse at a later time in history.

As we continue this study, we will see that this prophecy is presently being fulfilled. At this present time, Christ has purposed to go forth in the power of the Spirit *to conquer and vanquish His enemies* with even greater power and effectiveness than He did in the first century. We will discuss this in greater detail in chapter 6.

The Letter to Ephesus

On the day that He opened the first seal, besides the 120 who were praying in the upper room, 3,000 souls were ushered into the kingdom of God (see Acts 2:1–4). Afterward, history tells us that the church quickly grew in power and numbers for about sixty years—but toward the latter part of the first century, they began to grow complacent and drift away from their first love. Therefore, Jesus instructed John to write them a letter:

> To the angel of the church of Ephesus [full purposed] write, "These things says He who holds the seven stars in His right hand, who walks in the midst of the seven golden lampstands: I know your works, your labor, your patience, and that you cannot bear those who are evil. *And you have tested those who say they are apostles and are not, and have found them liars*; and you have persevered and have patience, and have labored for My name's sake and have not become weary. *Nevertheless I have this against you, that you have left your first love.* Remember therefore from where you have fallen; repent and do the first works, or else I will come to you quickly and remove your lampstand from its place—unless you repent. *But this you have, that you hate the deeds of the Nicolaitans, which I also hate.* He who has an ear, let him hear what the Spirit says to the

churches. To him who overcomes I will give to eat from the tree of life, which is in the midst of the Paradise of God." (Rev. 2:1–7; italics mine)

From this we can see that the early church heeded a warning that Paul previously gave the elders of Ephesus. He warned them that certain, selfish, ambitious men (false apostles) would arise within the church *speaking perverse things to draw away disciples after themselves* (see Acts 20:28–31). Besides judging and rejecting the false apostles, the Ephesians also despised those individuals who sought preeminence in the church and tried to dominate the brethren. This is signified by their hatred of the *deeds* of the *Nicolaitans*. This word is from *nikos* (meaning victorious, or to conquer) and *Laodikeus* (meaning common people, or laity), so Nicolaitan literally means to be "victorious over the people" (see 3 John 1:9–10). But hating and rejecting witchcraft control isn't enough to satisfy God. It is never enough to just hate evil. We must fervently love and be devoted to the One who chose us from the foundation of the world (see Mark 12:30; Ephesians 1:4).

The Red Horse (AD 100–313)

God is faithful to chastise and purify His saints who sin so that they will not be condemned with the ungodly (see Hebrews 12:5–11). The primary thing that He uses to purify His people is *affliction*. "Behold, I have refined you, but not as silver; I have tested you in the furnace of affliction" (Isa. 48:10). Therefore the Lamb opened the second seal, releasing war upon the world and persecution upon the church.

> When He opened the second seal, I heard the second living creature saying, "Come and see." Another horse, *fiery red*, went out. And it was granted to the one who sat on it to take peace from the earth, and that people should kill

one another; and there was given to him *a great sword*. (Rev. 6:3–4; italics mine)

The Letter to Smyrna

The fiery red horse (evil passion, i.e., hatred) and great sword both signify *persecution of the saints*. Christ addressed the issue of persecution in the second prophetic letter that He had previously dictated to John:

> And to the angel of the church in Smyrna [myrrh; i.e., incense] write, "These things says the First and the Last, who was dead, and came to life: I know your works, tribulation, and poverty (but you are rich); and I know the blasphemy of those who say they are Jews and are not, but are a synagogue of Satan. *Do not fear any of those things which you are about to suffer. Indeed, the devil is about to throw some of you into prison, that you may be tested, and you will have tribulation ten days. Be faithful until death, and I will give you the crown of life.* He who has an ear, let him hear what the Spirit says to the churches. He who overcomes shall not be hurt by the second death." (Rev. 2:8–11; italics mine)

Jesus taught that persecution is driven by hatred. This spirit wars against the church in three different ways—popular antagonism, intellectual assault, and physical harm and imprisonment. Popular antagonism is similar to the anti-Semitism that led to the Jewish Holocaust in Europe during World War II. This public sentiment is seen in America when the courts agree with citizens who sue others, who, for reasons of conscience, refuse to participate in their homosexual weddings. Thus, one can see that persecution is most effective when it is politicized, making Christian conduct illegal. In some countries, this includes criminalizing private meetings. Once matters of conscience are made illegal, persecution becomes *prosecution* instead of *persecution*. Once it is condoned and enforced by law, it becomes impossible to resist. The persecuted can only submit, hide, or flee.

On the other hand, *intellectual* assaults can have a positive benefit. These attacks cause men to search the Scriptures to defend their deeds and doctrines and disprove their critics. Many of the creeds and refined doctrines that we have today are the result of this type of persecution. Likewise, physical persecution, whether legal or illegal, helps purify the church—hirelings flee, and sincere Christians turn to the One who loves them enough to confront them in their lukewarmness.

Ten means to *test* or *measure*, thus the ten days of Smyrna's tribulation was symbolic of the entire time the early church was persecuted, which was about two hundred years. Persecution in the Roman empire was sporadic at first, beginning under the reign of emperor Nero (AD 54–68) and lasting until AD 313 when Constantine signed the Edict of Milan, ending persecution throughout the Roman state. Before this (in the last half of the third century), it was especially severe as successive Roman emperors sought to stamp out Christianity and restore Rome to her former glory.

The Black Horse (AD 313–1215)

Although persecution removes the half-hearted and fearful from the church, since it primarily targets the churches' leaders, it also imprisons or kills those who are defenders of the faith. Thus it removes those who are well educated in the word and understand the ways of God. This opens the door for heresy in doctrine and corruption in leadership to infiltrate the church. These two, heresy and internal corruption, were the second major problem confronting the church, making it necessary for the Lamb to open the third seal:

> When He opened the third seal, I heard the third living creature say, "Come and see." So I looked, and behold, *a black horse,* and he who sat on it had *a pair of scales* in his hand. And I heard a

> voice in the midst of the four living creatures saying, "A quart of wheat for a denarius, and three quarts of barley for a denarius; and *do not harm the oil and the wine.*" (Rev. 6:5–6; italics mine)

This course correction ended political persecution ("do not harm the oil and the wine"). It was almost a thousand years before widespread persecution arose again. Although stopping persecution was necessary (it had accomplished all that it was capable of doing), it left in its wake much doctrinal heresy and an open door for the Nicolaitans to gain power.

At this time, Constantine appointed himself as head over all the churches. Although he was biblically illiterate, he presided over all aspects of the church's doctrine and government. In Jesus' letter to this era, He specifically addressed *Satan's throne*, which as time transpired and the centuries unfolded became occupied by a secession of power-hungry bishops. Some of these later became known as "papa" (Latin for father, or *pope*).

The Letter to Pergamos

> And to the angel of the church in Pergamos [much marriage; i.e., in covenant with the world] write, "These things says He who has the sharp two-edged sword: I know your works, and where you dwell, *where Satan's throne is.* And you hold fast to My name, and did not deny My faith even in the days in which Antipas [anti-papa, i.e., anti-pope] was My faithful martyr, who was killed among you, where Satan dwells. But I have a few things against you, because you have there those who hold the doctrine of Balaam, who taught Balak to put a stumbling block before the children of Israel, to eat things sacrificed to idols, and to commit sexual immorality. *Thus you also have those who hold the doctrine of the Nicolaitans,*

which thing I hate. Repent, or else I will come to you quickly and will fight against them with the sword of My mouth. He who has an ear, let him hear what the Spirit says to the churches. To him who overcomes I will give some of the hidden manna to eat. And I will give him a white stone, and on the stone a new name written which no one knows except him who receives it." (Rev. 2:12–17; italics mine)

The days of Antipas, God's faithful martyr, refers to those who were killed because they opposed the Nicolaitans' takeover of the church. Antipas means *anti-papa*, (from *pater*, Latin for *father*). This refers to those who were martyred when they opposed the popish "one-man rule" which replaced the team ministry that Christ ordained and intended the church to be governed by (see Acts 13:1; 20:17, 28; Galatians 2:9).

That which began as *deeds* that both God and the saints hated and despised, now became the accepted *doctrine* of church government—*and still exists and persists as such unto this day!* Besides Constantine, church history records the progressive takeover of the churches by ambitious, power-hungry bishops, each striving to rule over a greater number of cities (unlike today, each city had only one church). The end of this epic power struggle cumulated with one bishop ruling over all the others. At this present time, the city-state where this single bishop resides is called the Vatican, and he is known as the pope.

Later, in the sixteenth century, Martin Luther would call the pope the Antichrist, and since *anti* actually means "in place of," in many ways the pope is just that, declaring himself as the vicar of Christ and assuming headship over the Catholic (meaning "universal") Church, a role belonging solely to Christ:

> And He [Christ] is the head of the body, the church, who is the beginning, the firstborn from the dead, that in all things He may have the preeminence. (Col. 1:18)

> And God has appointed these in the church: *first apostles, second prophets, third teachers*, after that miracles, then gifts of healings, helps, administrations, varieties of tongues. (1 Cor. 12:28; italics mine)

As for the power-hungry bishops who strove among themselves for supremacy, Jesus admonished His disciples against all such selfish ambition.

> And He [Jesus] said to them, "The kings of the Gentiles exercise lordship over them, and *those who exercise authority over them are called 'benefactors.' But not so among you*; on the contrary, he who is greatest among you, let him be as the younger, and he who governs as he who serves." (Luke 22:25–26; italics mine)

The perversion which Jesus said should "not [be] so among you" became the norm! From this point on, the *deeds* of the Nicolaitans that the early church abhorred and God still hates became the accepted *doctrine* of the church—as Jesus stated in His letter to those in Pergamos. Both doctrinally and spiritually, the black horse introduced a period of spiritual famine, fulfilling a prophesy that Amos gave hundreds of years before:

> "Behold, the days are coming," says the Lord GOD, "That I will send a famine on the land, *Not a famine of bread, Nor a thirst for water, But of hearing the words of the LORD*. They shall wander from sea to sea, and from north to east; They shall run to and fro, seeking the word of the LORD, but shall not find it. In that day the fair virgins and strong young men shall faint from thirst." (Amos 8:11–13; italics mine)

The church was weighed in the scales the black horse's rider carried and found wanting, resulting in famine wages. A denarius was a day's wages, and a measure of wheat was only enough for one meal, but three measures of barley was enough for three. The meaning? Wheat was the rich man's bread, and barley belonged to the poor. As Mary said, "He has filled the hungry with good things, And the rich He has sent away empty" (Luke 1:53). Those who were poor in spirit (humble) had bread enough, but the rich were sent away hungry. They were deprived of the Bread of Life. But as we will see, things had to get much worse before they would get any better.

The Pale Horse (AD 1215–1700)

Because God's eternal purpose is to "bring many sons into glory" (see Hebrews 2:10), the decadent condition of the church caused the Captain of their salvation to open the forth seal:

> When He opened the fourth seal, I heard the voice of the fourth living creature saying, "Come and see." So I looked, and behold, *a pale horse*. And the name of him who sat on it was Death, and Hades followed with him. And *power was given to them over a fourth of the earth,* to kill with *sword*, with *hunger*, with *death*, and by the *beasts* of the earth. (Rev. 6:7–8; italics mine)

In the twelfth century, Pope Gregory IX instituted the infamous papal inquisition and the sword of political persecution, which had ceased for almost a thousand years, resumed once again. This time it was the church who made matters of conscience illegal. It set up a powerful office to root out and punish what it deemed as heresy. Whole people groups were hunted down, and some were virtually eliminated during this time, including the Waldensians in Germany and Northern Italy and the Huguenots of France. The Catholic Inquisition lasted for several hundred years. Then, in 1478, the Spanish Inquisition began and lasted until Napoleon conquered Spain in 1808 and ordered the Inquisition there to be abolished.

It has been estimated that more than a million people were killed through these two inquisitions. The horrific injustices these people suffered and the way they were falsely accused, tortured, and burned to death began to open the people's eyes to the obvious fact that instead of representing God, the pope and his army of enforcers were the very epitome of evil! This abuse of papal authority began the slow process of preparing the people to embrace the reformation when it finally came.

In addition to the horror brought upon the world by the inquisition, in 1347, the "black death" (bubonic plague) arrived on the shores of Europe and by 1351 had decimated the population, killing as many as fifty million people. There were further outbreaks in the following decades until about one quarter of the world's population was destroyed (about sixty million out of an estimated population of 240 million). Because it reached into every segment of society, including the farming communities, it caused widespread famine throughout the known world. Thus death was caused by both the plague and severe food shortage. This natural famine was combined with the already existing spiritual famine for "hearing the word of the Lord," wreaking havoc and utter devastation throughout the known world.

During the time the black death ravaged England, one English cleric, William Langland, wrote, "God is deaf nowadays and will not hear us. And for our guilt he grinds good men to dust," echoing the prevailing sentiment of the times. There was much offence against the priests, many of whom fled their posts when faced with the plague's devastations. This, along with the obvious corruption and abuses within the Catholic Church, helped set the stage for the reformation.

Although, when necessary, God's chastisements are severe, they are always redemptive in their purpose. The pale horse's rider did not ride in vain. Change was on the horizon.

Chapter 4

The Reformation

THE LETTER TO THYATIRA

And to the angel of the church in Thyatira [odor of affliction] write, "These things says the Son of God, who has eyes like a flame of fire, and His feet like fine brass: I know your works, love, service, faith, and your patience; and as for your works, the last are more than the first [i.e., religious traditions and works had replaced their first love (works are listed before love)]. Nevertheless I have a few things against you, because *you allow that woman Jezebel, who calls herself a prophetess, to teach and seduce My servants to commit sexual immorality and eat things sacrificed to idols*. And I gave her time to repent of her sexual immorality, and she did not repent. *Indeed I will cast her into a sickbed, and those who commit adultery with her into great tribulation, unless they repent of their deeds.* I will kill her children with death, and all the churches shall know that I am He who searches the minds and hearts. And I will give to each one of you according to your works. Now to you I say, and to the rest in Thyatira, as many as do not have this doctrine, who have not known the depths of Satan, as they say, I will put on you no other burden. But hold fast what you have till I come. And he who overcomes, and keeps My works until the end, to him I will give power over the nations—he shall rule them with a rod of iron; They shall be dashed to pieces like the potter's vessels'—as I also have received from My Father [see Psalm 2:9]; and *I will give him the morning star.* He who has an ear, let him hear what the Spirit says to the churches." (Rev. 2:18–29; italics mine)

Although the world was in utter chaos and the church was completely estranged from its founder, hope was on its way. (We will discuss Jezebel in chapter 11 and 14). It is at this time in history that men began to question the church's supreme authority over every aspect of their lives and two reformations were birthed—one secular and one religious. The first, secular, reformation was the Renaissance (meaning *rebirth*), which began in the fourteenth century and lasted until the beginning of the seventeenth century. It helped spawn the second, Protestant (*protesters*), reformation, which officially began in AD 1517.

One thing that greatly aided the spread of the Protestant reformation was the invention of the Gutenberg printing press in AD 1450. This machine enabled the communication of ideas to spread far and wide and allowed the Bible to be put into the hands of the common people. For the first time in history, people could read the Bible for themselves. Therefore, many began to question the traditional doctrines and practices of the church and were able to see for themselves the error they had been led into. Many of Luther's numerous papers and Calvin's books and commentaries were printed and distributed throughout the land, influencing and encouraging many other reformers to take a stand against the corrupt practices of the church.

The Renaissance promoted the rediscovery of classical philosophy, literature, and art and the Protestant reformation the rediscovery of the first three foundational doctrines of the church. One was secular and the other spiritual, but both were welcomed by the common people and greatly opposed by worldly kings and ungodly priests. The Renaissance encouraged people to think for themselves, resulting in both scientific and political change and promoted economic growth and individual prosperity (although it also paved the way for Satan to introduce Darwin's theory of evolution to the world).

The Protestant reformation turned many of the people away from heresy and false worship, where Mary was hailed as the mediator between Christ and the people, and for all practical purposes, the church proclaimed itself as the savior instead of Jesus. In the letter to Thyatira quoted above, Jesus' promise to give the *morning star* to anyone who overcame Jezebel's deception refers to this heresy. *The morning star is Jesus!* (See Revelation 22:16.)

Instead of the fear of God, the people feared the pope because they believed that he had the power to excommunicate them and deprive them of eternal life. When the early reformers such as Luther and Calvin proclaimed Christ as Savior and taught the priesthood of every believer, they invoked the ire of the entire papal system against themselves.

The Letter to Sardis (1517)

As Christ's next letter reveals, many began to realize that the superstitious rituals and doctrines of demons that they had been subjected to by the unscrupulous papal system were fraudulent. Although they were known as Christians by their peers, they were unknown to Christ, and their ritualistic works of penance and repetitious prayers were unacceptable to God (see Matthew 6:7):

> And to the angel of the church in Sardis write, "These things says He who has the seven Spirits of God and the seven stars: I know your works, that *you have a name that you are alive,*

but you are dead. Be watchful, and strengthen the things which remain, that are ready to die, for I have not found your works perfect before God. Remember therefore how you have received and heard; hold fast and repent. Therefore if you will not watch, I will come upon you as a thief, and you will not know what hour I will come upon you. *You have a few names even in Sardis who have not defiled their garments; and they shall walk with Me in white, for they are worthy.* He who overcomes shall be clothed in white garments, and I will not blot out his name from the Book of Life; but I will confess his name before My Father and before His angels. He who has an ear, let him hear what the Spirit says to the churches." (Rev. 3:1–6; italics mine)

At this time the Lamb opened the fifth seal, revealing a prayer meeting going on in heaven and announcing a waiting period that continues to this day.

The Martyrs' Seal (1700–?)

All seven seals of the book of life are either creative or redemptive. Their actual purpose is to bring about repentance and turn the church back to its original purity and devotion to God, not to destroy mankind. So once the reformation started and the church began turning back to its first love, instead of bringing correction to a wayward church, the fifth seal announces a time of waiting: "For [God] does not afflict willingly, Nor grieve the children of men" (Lam. 3:33). Since the people were turning back to Him, He welcomed them with open arms. This seal also gives us an insight into the persecution that the saints endured in the past and that we ourselves can expect to endure in the near future. Satan will never cease to fight against the saints who love and worship God:

> When He opened the fifth seal, I saw under the altar the souls of those who had been slain for the word of God and for the testimony which they held. And they cried with a loud voice, saying, "How long, O Lord, holy and true, until You judge and avenge our blood on those who dwell on the earth?" Then a white robe was given to each of them; and it was said to them that they should rest a little while longer, until both the number of their fellow servants and their brethren, who would be killed as they were, was completed. (Rev. 6:9–11)

Why is God so patient with those who imprison and slaughter His people? Because their actions reveal the hidden thoughts and evil intents of their hearts—so that they may be judged accordingly—as Simeon prophesied to Mary, about Jesus' crucifixion:

> Then Simeon blessed them, and said to Mary His mother, "Behold, this Child is destined for the fall and rising of many in Israel, and for a sign which will be spoken against (yes, a sword [of grief] will pierce through your own soul also), that the thoughts of many hearts may be revealed." (Luke 2:34–35; also see John 7:19–20)

One of the results of the enlightenment taking place at that time in both the secular and spiritual world was that when Martin Luther began to expose and oppose the corrupt doctrines and practices of the church, many people were ready to hear his message and follow his lead. The resulting reformation was actually a long, arduous, *and progressive* process—lasting over four hundred years—and in many ways, it is still in process. The last three of the seven foundational doctrines are only now being restored, including the original church government (which was corrupted and taken over by power hungry bishops in the first and second centuries).

The first reformation restored the first three foundational doctrines—which primarily restored Christ as the Savior instead of the church proclaiming itself as savior. The second reformation, which we will discuss below, restored the Holy Spirit baptism with the laying on of hands, and the last reformation, which is just now in its beginning stages, will restore the full revelation of the Father's miraculous works and *His* government over the church (see Hebrews 6:1–2; Acts 2:42–43, 4:33; John 14:10).

As mentioned above, the fourth of the seven foundational doctrines, the doctrine of the laying on of hands, was restored in 1906 when the Holy Spirit was once again poured out as it was on the day of Pentecost. At that time, the second, parallel reformation was birthed and, like the first reformation, continues to unfold at this present time. This one is a progressive revelation of the baptism of the Holy Spirit and His various manifestations instead of a reformation of doctrine. This era of spiritual gifts and manifestations is addressed in Christ's next letter:

The Letter to Philadelphia (AD 1906)

And to the angel of the church in Philadelphia [brotherly love] write, "These things says He who is holy, He who is true, 'He who has the key of David, He who opens and no one shuts, and shuts and no one opens': I know your works. See, I have set before you an open door, and no one can shut it; for *you have a little strength, have kept My word, and have not denied My name.* Indeed I will make those of the synagogue of Satan, who say they are Jews and are not, but lie—indeed I will make them come and worship before your feet, and to know that I have loved you. Because you have kept My command to persevere, *I also will keep you from the hour of trial which shall come upon the whole world, to test those who dwell on the earth.* Behold, I am coming quickly! Hold fast what you have, that no one may take your crown. He who overcomes, I will make him a pillar in the temple of My God, and he shall go out no more. And I will write on him the name of My God and the name of the city of My God, the New Jerusalem, which comes down out of heaven from My God. And I will write on him My new name. He who has an ear, let him hear what the Spirit says to the churches." (Rev. 3:7–13; italics mine)

The latter-rain outpouring of the Holy Spirit that began in 1906 at 312 Azusa Street in Los Angeles, California, has spread around the world, spawning the fastest growing churches on the planet. Worldwide, by 1990, there were over 250 million Spirit-filled Christians. As the letter Jesus addressed to the Philadelphians acknowledged, the members of this apostolic church "have a little strength, have kept [His] word, and have not denied [His] name." However, there is a problem. Existing and expanding parallel with this Spirit-filled, *apostolic* church is an *apostate* church, which is also numbered in the millions. Jesus dictated a letter to John for this church which was addressed different than the other six letters. Instead of being addressed to the angel *in the city* the church was in, it is written directly to the messenger of the church members themselves.

THE LETTER TO THE LAODICEANS

Laodicean means "the people's choice." There is nothing about this church that Christ could commend! This apostate church chooses teachers who will tickle their ears and tell them what they want to hear (see 2 Timothy 4:4–5). The Holy Spirit is unwelcome and is forbidden to manifest Himself. Christ Himself isn't welcome unless He is willing to compromise His holiness and acknowledge them in their sin, which He will *never* do, and neither should we (see 1 Corinthians 14:39; Ephesians 5:5–15):

> And to the angel of the church of the Laodiceans [the people's choice; i.e., not God's will, but rather the people's will be done] write, "These things says the Amen, the Faithful and True Witness, the Beginning of the creation of God: I know your works, that you are neither cold nor hot. I could wish you were cold or hot. *So then, because you are lukewarm, and neither cold nor hot, I will vomit you out of My mouth.* Because you say, 'I am rich, have become wealthy, and have need of nothing'—*and do not know that you are wretched, miserable, poor, blind, and naked*—I counsel you to buy from Me gold refined in the fire, that you may be rich; and white garments, that you may be clothed, that the shame of your nakedness may not be revealed; and anoint your eyes with eye salve, that you may see. As many as I love, I rebuke and chasten. Therefore be zealous and repent. Behold, I stand [outside] at the door and knock. If anyone hears My voice and opens the door, I will come in to him and dine with him, and he with Me. To him who overcomes I will grant to sit with Me on My throne, as I also overcame and sat down with My Father on His throne. He who has an ear, let him hear what the Spirit says to the churches." (Rev. 3:14–22; italics mine)

Obviously, and sadly, this condition exists in many churches throughout the world. Christ will not tolerate a bride who loves this present world and only serves him for the material benefits. Those who worship the golden calf of prosperity will soon be vomited out (see Exodus 32:7–8; 1 John 2:15–16).

Knowing and understanding this, we should take heed and learn from our predecessors' failures. Christ's rebuke to the churches may be summed up in the following seven admonitions, which we will do well to consider and apply to ourselves. Therefore we should

1. repent and return to our first love, who is the Lord Jesus Christ, rather than justifying and placating ourselves by our own religious works (see Mark 12:30);
2. repent for practicing the doctrine of Balaam, which, among other things, is essentially merchandising the gifts, that is, "peddling the gospel" (see 2 Corinthians 2:17; 2 Peter 2:15; Numbers 22:7);
3. repent for departing from the original model of the saints ministering to one another in love. (The saints have become slothful and willingly allowed those who practice the deeds and doctrine of the Nicolaitans, which God hates, to do all the ministering instead of the saints doing it themselves.) See 1 Peter 4:10; Ephesians 4:15–16; 1 Corinthians 12:7–11, 14:1, 24–26; James 5:16;
4. repent for allowing the spirit of Jezebel into our homes and marriages, deceiving and seducing us into practicing idolatry and sexual immorality, including no-fault divorce and remarriage (see Colossians 3:5; Matthew 5:32);
5. repent for not walking in love. Our works must measure up to Christ's standard, which is to love our neighbors as ourselves (see James 2:8);
6. repent for being proud, self-sufficient, and self-righteous, which blinds our eyes to our own nakedness and spiritual poverty; and
7. repent for being complacent and lukewarm, choosing to please ourselves instead of seeking God's will for our lives.

One wise church historian wrote, "Every major heresy started with a minor deviation from the truth." Both the reformation of doctrine and of spirituality are incomplete. The church still has some doctrinal errors that are accepted as truth, and many churches are seriously deficient in ministering the spirit—and the original pattern and full complement of biblical, team ministry in church government hasn't been restored, either—the government signified by the prophet, priest, and king of the Old Testament and exemplified by the apostle, prophet, and pastor-teacher of the New hasn't been fully restored and put into operation. The church still has some restructuring to do and some course corrections to make.

The third reformation, which is progressively unfolding now, will bring every error to light and everything that has been lost will be fully restored. The message of impending judgment contained in the next seal is preparing the way for Christ's return and will bring correction to both the church and the world. "He who has an ear, let him hear what the Spirit [is saying] to the churches."

Chapter 5

The Sixth Seal

The Announcement of the Coming, Great
Day of the Lord (AD 2001–Present)

The deplorable condition of the apostate, worldwide, Laodicean church makes it necessary for the Lamb to open the sixth seal. This seal sets the stage for the restoration of all things prophesied from the beginning of time to be fulfilled and brought to fruition, including the second coming of Christ (see Acts 3:20–21):

> I looked when He opened the sixth seal, and behold, there was a *great earthquake*; and the *sun* became *black as sackcloth of hair*, and the *moon* became like *blood*. And the *stars* of heaven fell to the earth, as a fig tree drops its *late figs* when it is shaken by *a mighty wind*. Then the *sky receded* as a scroll when it is rolled up, and every *mountain* and *island* was *moved out of its place*. And the kings of the earth, the great men, the rich men, the commanders, the mighty men, every slave and every free man, hid themselves in the caves and in the rocks of the mountains, and said to

> the mountains and rocks, "Fall on us and hide us from the face of Him who sits on the throne and from the wrath of the Lamb! For the great day of His wrath has come, and who is able to stand?" (Rev. 6:12–17; italics mine)

There is a tremendous amount of symbolism contained in the sixth seal. With God's help, we will attempt to interpret each symbol individually. The first one, a great earthquake, is symbolic of *great shaking and change*. It is God's way of breaking down and destroying everything that resists His will. Since all of the seals are redemptive, the earthquake's purpose is to remove temporary things and establish things that are eternal, as stated in Hebrews 12:

> See that you do not refuse Him who speaks. For if they did not escape who refused Him who spoke on earth, much more shall we not escape if we turn away from Him who speaks from heaven, whose voice then shook the earth; but now He has promised, saying, "*Yet once more I shake not only the earth, but also heaven.*" Now this, "Yet once more," indicates the removal of those things that are being shaken, as of things that are made, *that the things which cannot be shaken may remain.* (Heb. 12:25–27; italics mine)

Thus the purpose of the great earthquake that was released when the Lamb opened the sixth seal is to reveal and remove that which is noncompliant with His will and purposes. This is where we are now! *We are presently at this juncture of Revelation's time line.* Unlike the first four seals, the fifth and sixth seals are opened in close proximity to one another. The fifth seal announces a waiting period, and the sixth reveals what transpires during that space of time. We will see that everything that John saw in those two seals is either being released now or will be released in the near future. Although the "last days" began at Pentecost, we are now in the "latter days" spoken of in Scripture (see Acts 2:17–18; Isaiah 2:2). An example of a latter-day scripture is quoted below:

> The anger of the LORD will not turn back Until He has executed and performed the thoughts of His heart. In the latter days you will understand it perfectly. (Jer. 23:20)

The sixth seal was broken, and the release of its contents began with the 9/11/2001 terrorist attack upon the World Trade Center towers in New York City. The message is in the date—9 means *harvest*, and 11 means *end*, 2,000 means to *divide or judge, using mature judgment*, and 1 means *beginning*—thus the actual date is a declaration to the world that *the time has come for the end-time harvest of judgment to begin* (see Joel 3:13; Revelation 14:18). This attack was a sign to the whole world, and although the prophecy quoted below begins with the fall of the towers, like the scroll's sixth seal, it will take several decades to be completely fulfilled. But we can see that much of it is already in the process of fulfillment:

> There will be on every high mountain And on every high hill Rivers and streams of waters, In the day of the great slaughter, *When the towers fall.* Moreover the light of the *moon* will be as the light of the sun, And the light of the *sun* will be sevenfold, As the light of seven days, In the day that the LORD binds up the bruise of His people And heals the stroke of their wound. Behold, the name of the LORD comes from afar, Burning with His anger, And His burden is heavy; His lips are full of indignation, And His tongue like a devouring fire. His breath is like an overflowing stream, Which reaches up to the neck, To sift the nations with the sieve of futility; And there shall be a bridle in the jaws of the people, Causing them to err. (Isaiah 30:25–28; italics mine)

The "rivers and streams of waters" are in reference of the Holy Spirit outpouring that is now being poured out upon the church. The "day of the great slaughter" Isaiah spoke of is the same as "the day of vengeance of our God" which is in reference to the judicial aspect of Christ's ministry (see Isaiah 61:2). We will discuss Isaiah's prophecy in greater detail later. The "day of vengeance," which unfolds in several stages, is now on God's agenda, as the latter part of the sixth seal proclaims, "For the great day of His wrath has come, and who is able to stand?"

The constant threat of worldwide terrorism, prolonged droughts, severe floods, vast locus swarms, raging wild fires, severe food shortages, deadly plagues, earthquakes in unexpected locations, powerful, record-breaking hurricanes and tornadoes, economic instability, social unrest, violent street riots and public protests and demonstrations, and sword rattling among nations along with the imminent threat of nuclear war, these are all part of this mighty earthquake.

Along with the changes brought about by the natural things being shaken, there are major spiritual changes on the horizon. The biblical principle of *first the natural and then the spiritual* is being followed even in this arena, as we will see as we continue this discussion (see 1 Corinthians 15:46).

The next thing John saw was the *sun*, which "became black as sackcloth of hair." The sun is a symbol for *God*, as in Psalm 84:11, "For the Lord God is a sun and shield." Among other things *black* is synonymous with darkness, as in Proverbs 7:9, "In the twilight, in the evening, In the *black and dark night*" (italics mine). And *sackcloth* is the cloth of *grief*, and *sorrow*, as in Genesis 37:34, "And Jacob rent his clothes, and put sackcloth upon his loins, and mourned for his son many days." Lastly, *hair* represents a *covering*, indicating that the sun (God) is completely covered and clothed with grief and mourning.

Putting this all together reveals that God is once again sorry and grieved within Himself for making man, in the same way that He was grieved in the days of Noah. But this time, instead of destroying them with water, He has determined to use fire!

> And the LORD was sorry that He had made man on the earth, and He was grieved in His heart. (Gen. 6:6)

The sixth seal exactly parallels another of Isaiah's astonishing prophesies. The symbols that Isaiah used are the same as those in Revelation:

> Behold, the day of the LORD comes, Cruel, with both wrath and fierce anger, To lay the land desolate; And *He will destroy its sinners from it.* For the stars of heaven and their constellations Will not give their light; *The sun will be darkened* in its going forth, And the moon will not cause its light to shine. "I will punish the world for its evil, And the wicked for their iniquity; I will halt the arrogance of the proud, And will lay low the haughtiness of the terrible. *I will make a mortal more rare than fine gold,* A man more than the golden wedge of Ophir. Therefore *I will shake the heavens, And the earth will move out of her place,* In the wrath of the LORD of hosts And in the day of His fierce anger." (Isa. 13:9–13; italics mine)

Continuing with our breakdown of the symbols in Revelation 6:12–17, we come to "and the moon became like blood." The moon is symbolic of the church. The saints sit in heavenly places with Christ, beholding the light of the sun, reflecting it down to a world clothed in darkness (see Ephesians 2:6; Matthew 5:14). From the beginning of creation, God's intention was for the church to rule over the night the same as Christ rules over the day (see John 9:5):

> Then God made two great lights: the greater light to rule the day [the sun. i.e., God in Christ], and the lesser light to rule the night [the moon: i.e., the church]. He made the stars also [the

> saints such as Abraham, Moses, Peter, Paul and Luther—see Hebrews 11:17–40]. God set them in the firmament of the heavens to give light on the earth, and to rule over the day and over the night, and to divide the light from the darkness. And God saw that it was good. (Gen. 1:16–18)

The moon "became like blood" is symbolic of martyrdom. This symbol forecasts the resurgence of persecution that Christ instructed the martyred saints in heaven to wait for, as we saw when the fifth seal was opened. Persecution of the saints is increasing at a phenomenal rate in many nations at this present time, which is one sign among many that confirms that we are in the midst of the opening of the sixth seal.

After this, John saw "the *stars of heaven* [as they] fell to the earth, as a fig tree drops its late figs when it is shaken by a mighty wind." Although many believe that *stars* are symbolic of angels (and in a few scriptures they are—as in Job 38:4–7), but the majority of time they are symbolic of people, specifically the elect saints of God. For instance, when Abraham was shown the stars and challenged to count them, God told him, "So shall your descendants be" (see Genesis 15:5; also Nehemiah 9:23).

When Joseph had a dream that the sun, moon, and eleven stars bowed down to him, Jacob correctly interpreted the eleven stars as Joseph's brothers (although at that time, there were only ten. Benjamin was born after Joseph was sold into slavery—see Genesis 37:9–10). And in one of the most important scriptures relevant to our study, Daniel was told by an angel that in the resurrection, "they that be wise shall shine as the brightness of the firmament; and they that turn many to righteousness as the stars for ever and ever" (Dan. 12:3).

We will see that the correct interpretation of stars as symbolic of saints rather than always meaning angels is very important later on in our study. Previously, we saw that *blood* represented *persecution*, and in this passage, we see that falling stars represent saints who are persecuted and tried. Although Daniel's vision quoted below is for a later time (though how much later, is uncertain), his vision explains John's vision of the stars falling:

> Those who do wickedly against the [gospel] covenant he shall corrupt with flattery; but the people who know their God shall be strong, and carry out great exploits. *And those of the people who understand shall instruct many; yet for many days they shall fall by sword and flame, by captivity and plundering.* Now when they fall, they shall be aided with a little help; but many shall join with them by intrigue. *And some of those of understanding shall fall, to refine them, purify them, and make them white*, until the time of the end; because it is still for the appointed time. (Dan. 11:32–35; italics mine)

The *mighty wind* that shakes the fig tree and causes its late figs to drop is the *spirit of sorcery*, which is the Antichrist spirit. John said that it was already working against the church when he wrote his first epistle (see 1 John 4:3). This spirit, which Paul said is the enemy of all righteousness, is working mightily in and through America's government at this present time (see Acts 13:8–10).

The spirit of sorcery controls and consumes the life of its victims solely for the edification of the sorcerer (see 1 Kings 21:5–16). This wind is blowing hard against Christ's true church in these latter days (*late* figs). Satan is furious because he knows that his time is short and that he will soon be imprisoned for a thousand years (more on this later).

The next line contains the symbols of the sky receding like a rolled-up scroll ("Then the sky receded as a scroll when it is rolled up"). The *sky* is symbolic for heaven (i.e., the church), and *receded* (Greek: *apochorizo*) actually means to *rend* apart or *split asunder*, so John saw the sky torn, *or split asunder*, then rolled up as a scroll is rolled up when the reading is finished and it is put away. This prophecy is a direct reference to God's end-time promise to shake both the earth and the heavens:

> "Yet once more I shake not only the earth, but also heaven." Now this, "Yet once more," *indicates the removal of those things that are being shaken*, as of things that are made, that the things which cannot be shaken may remain. (Heb. 12:26–27; italics mine)

This severe shaking will birth the third reformation, which we previously discussed. This third, and final, reformation will fulfill a prophecy that John the Baptist gave when he prophesied to the Jews about Messiah coming—the outpouring of the baptism of fire!

> John answered, saying to all, "I indeed baptize you with water; but One mightier than I is coming, whose sandal strap I am not worthy to loose. *He will baptize you with the Holy Spirit and fire.* His *winnowing fan is in His hand*, and He will thoroughly clean out His threshing floor, and gather the wheat into His barn; but the *chaff He will burn with unquenchable fire.*" (Luke 3:16–17; italics mine)

The outpouring of God's *baptism of fire* is going to change the existing church in much the same way the Catholic church was split asunder by the Protestant reformation in the sixteenth and seventeenth centuries. Likewise, many churches split over the Holy Spirit baptism when it was initially introduced in the early 1900s. This next twofold baptism, which will restore power, purity, and the fear of God to the church, will be no different!

During the flood, the windows of heaven were opened, and the rains poured out upon the earth, executing God's just judgments upon the world. Instead of a *baptism of water*, as that judgment was,

God's second ("Yet once more") outpouring of judgment will be a *baptism of fire*.

God's purifying fire will first be visited upon the church before it is poured out upon the world. Peter said that judgment begins at the house of God (1 Pet. 4:17). And Paul said that fire will try every man's works, of what sort they are (1 Cor. 3:13). Likewise, concerning the saints themselves, Jesus said, "For everyone will be seasoned with fire, and every sacrifice will be seasoned with salt (Mark 9:49).

The scroll being *rolled up* is symbolic of a complete change of God's heavenly agenda. Those who are spiritually sensitive realize that a major change is on the horizon. There is a paradigm shift on God's agenda—*both in the governmental structure of the church and in its function*. Change is coming, and coming soon! It will be mandated by the Spirit, and all that resist His mandate will be swept aside by the "winnowing fan [that] is in His hand" (see Luke 3:16–17).

The present church *will split asunder* as God pours out His new wine, simply because we have been so tardy and reluctant to change our ways and make Him a new wineskin. Our old religious traditions and programs cannot contain or sustain what's coming. Much of the persecution and shaking prophesied by John will come from the established church, which has, does, and always will resist and fight against God's new wine. Even some of the Pentecostal churches will balk and fight against the required changes, especially the restoration of proper, biblical, team ministry in church government.

Next, "And every mountain and island was moved out of its place." Later we will see that instead of them being moved, they completely disappear. What are mountains symbolic of? Mountains represent things that are *exalted*. Powerful, influential nations and kingdoms, such as America, Russia, and China, are mountains. And islands? Small, relatively insignificant nations, such as those that are actually islands, as Cuba and Trinidad, or those standalone, independent nations such as Venezuela and Costa Rica, are islands.

Being moved "out of their places" is symbolic of the balance of power shifting, such as major changes in their economic prosperity or military strength and alliances. For example, during WWII, America was allied with England, Australia, Russia, and China. Our enemies were Japan, Germany, and Italy. Now our enemies are Russia and China, and those friendly to us include Germany, Italy, and Japan!

Economically, during and immediately after World War Two, the United States became the greatest lender on earth. Now she is the greatest borrower. Her national debt is presently growing at an ever-increasing, unsustainable rate. Likewise, Venezuela was once the richest of all the Central American nations; now she is the poorest! Russia and China are both moving toward a capitalistic economy while America is shifting toward socialism.

Why is everything shifting? Because God uses man's own weapons to chastise man, and God's end-time scenario will turn man's own sword against himself. God is over all kingdoms and nations, and He aligns them according to His own will and purposes:

> The LORD has established His throne in heaven, And His kingdom rules over all. (Ps. 103:19)

> The king's heart is in the hand of the LORD, Like the rivers of water; He turns it wherever He wishes. (Prov. 21:1)

The rest of this seal is a declaration of God's impending wrath upon the ungodly. It includes the seven classifications of mankind: kings, great men, rich men, commanders, mighty men, slaves, and free men. No one will be spared the wrath to come whose name is not written in the Lamb's book of life. This advanced prophetic proclamation is like Jonah's warning to Nineveh. If the nations repent and turn to God, there will be a delay; if not, God's promised wrath is soon to come:

> And the kings of the earth, the great men, the rich men, the commanders, the mighty men, every slave and every free man, hid themselves in the caves and in the rocks of the mountains, and said to the mountains and rocks, "Fall on us

and hide us from the face of Him who sits on the throne and from the wrath of the Lamb! For the great day of His wrath has come, and who is able to stand?" (Rev. 6:15–17)

The sixth seal's message may be summed up and paraphrased this way—during the waiting period announced by the fifth seal (where God's avenging judgment is delayed until many more saints are killed), God is once again sorry and grieved over having made mankind, the same as He was in the days of Noah (see Genesis 6:6; Luke 17:26–30). Therefore, *the spirit of Antichrist* (and later, the Antichrist himself) is unleashed as a mighty wind upon the church to expose and remove lukewarm, insincere "believers" and to season the remnant with fire. Both heaven and earth are being shaken to remove everything that isn't acceptable to God in the church and to reposition and rearrange the nations for the judgment to come. During this time, many saints are suffering affliction and persecution as their faith is tried and tested, as Christ works to purify His bride in preparation for His glorious return and the fiery judgment to follow.

During the relatively short waiting period that is offered by the fifth seal, and the progressive unfolding of the events of the sixth, the church must fulfill its commission to go into all the world and gather in the final harvest of souls that God has determined to save. We will discuss this final end-gathering in chapter 11:

> Therefore be patient, brethren, until the coming of the Lord. See how the farmer waits for the precious fruit of the earth, waiting patiently for it until it receives the early and latter rain. (Jas. 5:7)

Chapter 6

Open Heavens

God is opening the heavens to reveal and mandate a paradigm shift of the church's vision, structure, and function because the existing religious programs and traditions cannot contain or sustain that which is coming. Likewise, there is a divinely orchestrated, progressive realignment of the nations taking place—politically, socially, economically, and militarily—in preparation for His coming judgments.

Almost two thousand years ago, the church was birthed, and the gospel was launched by the white horse and its rider—the Holy Spirit and Jesus Christ, the powerful, conquering King! Now, in these last days, He is riding once again, fulfilling the prophetic promise and purpose that we saw in the first seal. As in the first century, He is now riding forth in the power of the Spirit *to conquer* His enemies and make them His footstool! In the following scripture, John said that "He who sat on [the white horse] was called Faithful and True, and in righteousness He judges and makes war":

> And I [John] fell at his [the angels] feet to worship him. But he said to me, "See that you do not do that! I am your fellow servant, and of your brethren who have the testimony of Jesus. Worship God! *For the testimony of Jesus is the spirit*

of prophecy." Now I saw heaven opened, and behold, a white horse. And He who sat on him was called Faithful and True, and in righteousness He judges and makes war. His eyes were like a flame of fire, and on His head were many crowns. He had a name written that no one knew except Himself. He was clothed with a robe dipped in blood, and His name is called The Word of God. And the armies in heaven, clothed in fine linen, white and clean, followed Him on white horses. Now out of His mouth goes a sharp sword, that with it He should strike the nations. And He Himself will rule them with a rod of iron. He Himself treads the winepress of the fierceness and wrath of Almighty God. And He has on His robe and on His thigh a name written: King of kings and Lord of lords. (Rev. 19:10–16; italics mine)

To see this from a proper perspective and place it in its historical time line, we must examine a particular incidence that occurred early in Jesus' ministry:

> Philip found Nathanael and said to him, "We have found Him of whom Moses in the law, and also the prophets, wrote—Jesus of Nazareth, the son of Joseph." And Nathanael said to him, "Can anything good come out of Nazareth?" Philip said to him, "Come and see." Jesus saw Nathanael coming toward Him, and said of him, "Behold, an Israelite indeed, in whom is no deceit!" Nathanael said to Him, "How do You know me?" Jesus answered and said to him, "Before Philip called you, when you were under the fig tree, I saw you." Nathanael answered and said to Him, "Rabbi, You are the Son of God! You are the King of Israel!" Jesus answered and said to

> him, "*Because I said to you, 'I saw you under the fig tree,' do you believe? You will see greater things than these.*" And He said to him, "Most assuredly, I say to you, *hereafter you shall see heaven open, and the angels of God ascending and descending upon the Son of Man.*" (John 1:45–51; italics mine)

Because Nathanael believed Jesus when He prophesied to him, He told him that he would see greater things than personal prophecy—he would see heaven opened and angels ministering to Christ. Likewise, because the remnant church has received and embraced the office and ministry of the prophet and the manifestations of the Holy Spirit, they are qualified to experience *open heavens and the ministry of angels,* as Jesus promised Nathanael.

Why are the angels ministering to the church instead of directly to Christ Himself? Because the church *is* the body of Christ! When the angels ascend and descend as they minister to the church, they are ministering to Christ's body! Notice the following reference to prophetic ministry in the verse immediately before John saw heaven opened:

> And I [John] fell at [the angels] feet to worship him. But he said to me, "See that you do not do that! I am your fellow servant, and of your brethren who have the testimony of Jesus. Worship God! *For the testimony of Jesus is the spirit of prophecy.*" *Now I saw heaven opened,* and behold, a white horse. And He who sat on him was called Faithful and True, and in righteousness He judges and makes war. (Rev. 19:10–11; italics mine)

"The testimony of Jesus is the spirit of prophecy"! And what is the "testimony of Jesus"? Jesus said, "We speak what We know and testify what We have seen" (John 3:11). So Christ's testimony is summed up in this verse: "I am He who lives, and was dead, and behold, I am alive forevermore. Amen. And I have the keys of Hades and of Death" (Rev. 1:18). Thus the spirit of prophecy testifies that He who once was dead, now lives "according to the power of an endless life" (see Hebrews 7:16). *The spirit of prophecy releases resurrection power to rule over the darkness of this world, pronounce judgment upon the wicked, and wage victorious warfare against Christ's many enemies!*

Up until now the priesthood of the Lamb has been faithfully administered by the church as it has struggled to publish the gospel throughout the earth. But now it is time for those who are sitting in heavenly places with Christ to embrace a paradigm shift in their thinking. It's time for the saints to rule, judge, and wage warfare with Christ. It's time to conduct holy war, and Christ is asking for volunteers!

> Who will rise up for me against the evildoers? Who will stand up for me against the workers of iniquity? (Ps. 94:16)
>
> The Lord said to my Lord, "Sit at My right hand, *Till I make Your enemies Your footstool.*" The Lord shall send the rod of Your strength out of Zion. Rule in the midst of Your enemies! *Your people shall be volunteers In the day of Your power*; In the beauties of holiness, from the womb of the morning, You have the dew of Your youth. (Ps. 110:1–3; italics mine)

Now is the day of Christ's power. *Now* is the time to join Christ's volunteer army and prepare for war. It's time to fight! David said Jesus isn't returning until the church makes Christ's enemies His footstool. Paul also prophesied of this time: "And the God of peace will crush Satan under your feet shortly" (Rom. 16:20). The fulfillment of Paul's "shortly" is at hand. Malachi is another prophet who foretold of these days:

> But to you who fear My name The Sun of Righteousness shall arise With healing in His

> wings; And you shall go out And grow fat like stall-fed calves. *You shall trample the wicked, For they shall be ashes under the soles of your feet On the day that I do this,* Says the LORD of hosts. (Mal. 4:2–3; italics mine)
>
>> Let God arise, Let His enemies be scattered;
>> Let those also who hate Him flee before Him.
>> (Ps. 68:1)

Jesus' initial introduction of the church was in reference to war. He said the gates of hell would not prevail against it, implying that war was inevitable (see Matthew 16:18).

In the same way that Moses led the descendants of Abraham to freedom, even so God, through the sacrificial offering of the Lamb, has liberated us from the power of darkness and translated us into the kingdom of His dear Son. Because we are sons, we each have an inheritance bestowed upon us. Moses only led Israel to freedom. It took the ministry of Joshua to lead them in war to actually *possess* their inheritance. Although the Lamb has indeed given us freedom, it will take the ministry of the mighty Lion of Judah to lead us to victory, and our inheritance lies on the other side of victory! We have to fight! Jesus said,

> And from the days of John the Baptist until now the kingdom of heaven suffers violence, and the violent take it by force. (Matt. 11:12)

The violent warfare Jesus refers to here is not the saints contending with God for their inheritance but rather contending with the enemy of our souls. God is fighting with and for us, not against us! Jesus said, "Do not fear, little flock, for it is your Father's good pleasure to give you the kingdom" (Luke 12:32).

Because Abraham obeyed God, he obtained the title deed to Canaan, which he left as an inheritance to Isaac and his descendants. Likewise, Jesus fully obeyed His heavenly Father and obtained every positive promise of the Old Testament, which through His death on the cross He has left as an inheritance to those who become His brothers and sisters through the adoption. When He arose from the dead, He became the firstborn of many brethren. As the firstborn, He received a double portion of the inheritance, thus giving Him the preeminence (see Deuteronomy 21:15–17; Colossians 1:18).

Israel's natural inheritance was and is the land of Canaan. Other than the land of Canaan, which exclusively belongs to the Jews, our inheritance consists of every positive promise contained in the Old Testament, both natural and spiritual, tangible and intangible. Everything from eternal life to physical healing—from financial prosperity to victory in warfare—nothing is excluded. Paul said,

> For the Son of God, Jesus Christ, who was preached among you by us—by me, Silvanus, and Timothy—was not Yes and No, but in Him was Yes. *For all the promises of God in Him are Yes, and in Him Amen,* to the glory of God through us. (2 Cor. 1:19–20; italics mine)

God was glorified when He fought for the Israelites and originally gave them possession of their land. He is glorified now when He fights for the little nation of Israel and gives them victory, as He did in 1967 during the six-day war, at the reunification of Jerusalem. Likewise, He is glorified when He gives us victory over the demonic forces that resist us and attempt to deprive us of our rightful inheritance, which is "the fullness of the blessings of the Gospel of Christ" (Rom. 15:29).

The war that we are now fighting is on two fronts. We first have to defeat Satan in our own life before we can legitimately avenge the disobedience of the world. Paul said,

> For though we walk in the flesh, we do not war according to the flesh. For the weapons of our warfare are not carnal but mighty in God for pulling down strongholds, casting down arguments and every high thing that exalts itself

against the knowledge of God, bringing every thought into captivity to the obedience of Christ, and *being ready to punish all disobedience when your obedience is fulfilled.* (2 Cor. 10:3–6; italics mine)

Likewise, Peter said that the world's judgment begins with us:

> For the time has come for judgment to begin at the house of God; and if it begins with us first, what will be the end of those who do not obey the gospel of God? (1 Pet. 4:17)

So the war on the home front is the place to start.

Chapter 7

War in Heaven

And *war broke out in heaven*: Michael and his angels fought with the dragon; and the dragon and his angels fought, but they did not prevail, nor was a place found for them in heaven any longer. *So the great dragon was cast out*, that serpent of old, called the Devil and Satan, who deceives the whole world; *he was cast to the earth, and his angels were cast out with him.* Then I heard a loud voice saying in heaven, "Now salvation, and strength, and the kingdom of our God, and the power of His Christ have come, for the accuser of our brethren, who accused them before our God day and night, has been cast down." (Rev. 12:7–10; italics mine)

Before we discuss this passage of scripture, we need to clear up a long-held misunderstanding about it. John is *not* talking about Satan being cast out of heaven into the Garden of Eden. John was instructed to "write the things which you have seen, and the things which are, and the things which will take place after this" (Rev. 1:1). The fall of Satan, that happened in the beginning, occurred thousands of years before John wrote Revelation.

So the first thing we need to ask ourselves is this: How did Satan get into heaven in the first place? Who let him in? Is there more than one heaven, and if so, which heaven does John refer to? The correct answer to these questions may surprise you.

First, there are several heavens, as the first chapter of Genesis shows us, although they are easily overlooked. We know that in the beginning God created the heaven and the earth. Then, on the second day, He created a firmament which He also called heaven. So here we clearly have two separate heavens. In addition to those two, Paul said that he knew a man who was caught up to the *third* heaven, so there are at least three, confirmed, heavens in Scripture. The heaven that John referred to in Revelation 12 is the second heaven, since the third heaven is called the paradise of God, and nothing that defiles can enter there. Also, the third heaven is the heaven that Satan was cast down from in the beginning (see Genesis 1:1–8, 3:14–15; 2 Corinthians 12:2–4).

So how does Satan gain access to the second heaven? Sadly, the answer is the saints invite him in! Satan has no audience with God without a mediator. The man born blind that Jesus healed said, "Now we know that God does not hear [unrepentant] sinners; but if anyone is a worshiper of God and does His will, He hears him" (John 9:31).

Satan neither worships God nor does His will, so unless one of those who sit in heavenly places with Christ speaks for him, he cannot accuse anyone. The way he is overcome and cast out is for the saints to humble themselves and cease finding fault with one another. We must learn to excuse rather than accuse each other:

> Therefore submit to God. Resist the devil and he will flee from you... Humble yourselves in the sight of the Lord, and He will lift you up. Do not speak evil of one another, brethren... Who are you to judge another? (Jas. 4:7, 10–12)

Paul asked the same question, "Who are you to judge another's servant? To his own master he stands or falls" (Rom. 14:4). When the saints cease to "speak evil of another brethren," Satan is silenced. David gives us more understanding and detailed instructions about this battle in one of his psalms:

> But *to the wicked* God says: "What right have you to declare My statutes, *Or take My covenant in your mouth*, Seeing you hate instruction And cast My words behind you? *When you saw a thief, you consented with him*, And have been a partaker with adulterers. You give your mouth to evil, And your tongue frames deceit. *You sit and speak against your brother; You slander your own mother's son.* These things you have done, and I kept silent; *You thought that I was altogether like you;* But I will rebuke you, And set them in order before your eyes. Now consider this, you who forget God, Lest I tear you in pieces, And there be none to deliver: *Whoever offers praise glorifies Me*; And to him who orders his conduct aright I will show the salvation of God." (Ps. 50:16–23; italics mine)

The *wicked* that David refers to in this psalm isn't the sinners of the world. He is talking about those who call themselves children of God! Sinners don't take God's covenant in their mouths—they don't even know what His covenant is; nor do they declare His statutes—Christians do! It's Christians who are (unknowingly) consenting with the thief. What are they agreeing to? What is the thief stealing? Satan is stealing the saints' honor and reputation. When we criticize others and speak demeaning and derogatory things about them, we are destroying their reputations and heaping shame and disgrace upon them.

The horrific thing about this is that God stays silent. He doesn't say anything. He lets us have enough rope to hang ourselves! He said, "You sit and speak against your brother; You slander your own mother's son. These things you have done, and I kept silent; You thought that I was altogether like you." In our self-righteous smugness, we think that God agrees with us!

Christians are seated in heavenly places with Christ, who is the judge of all the earth. When we are speaking evil of one another, we are in the presence of the throne of God. Our accusations bring trials upon our brethren the same way Satan's accusations against Job brought severe trials upon him, causing him, through faith, to have to prove the sincerity of his love (see Job 1:6–12, 2:1–8).

The alarming part of this is that once those we have spoken evil of prove their faithfulness, then we have to go through the same tests and trials that we've brought upon them! Those who accused Daniel had to feed the lions the day after Daniel left the lion's den! Beware!

So what should we do? We must learn to guard our mouths and carefully consider what we say about one another. We must compliment and praise instead of criticize, justify instead of condemn, and excuse instead of accuse. In the Psalm quoted above, God said, "Whoever offers praise glorifies Me." He isn't talking about the saints praising Himself. The context clearly shows that He is talking about them complementing and praising one another! When we do that, Satan is completely defeated and cast down, and God is glorified.

John said that we can't hate our brother and say we love God, since our brother is made in the image of God (see 1 John 4:20). Likewise, when we find fault and criticize our brethren, we are finding fault and criticizing their creator—God Himself—*and it is not wise to criticize God!*

When the saints come into unity against Satan and cease to mediate for him, the way will finally be made for what we've been praying for—a mighty outpouring of God's Spirit and power:

> Then I heard a loud voice saying in heaven, *"Now salvation, and strength, and the kingdom of our God, and the power of His Christ have come,"* for the accuser of our brethren, who accused them before our God day and night, has been cast down." (Rev. 12:10; italics mine)

Chapter 8

Rejoicing in Victory

In the preceding chapter, we discussed the war that is going on in heaven and the important, indispensable step that the saints must take to be victorious on the home front—to come into unity and cease criticizing and condemning one another. But once the saints cease to lend their tongues to Satan and he is cast down from heaven, we have to defeat him on the second battleground, here on the earth.

> And they [the saints] overcame him by the blood of the Lamb and by the word of their testimony, and they did not love their lives to the death. *Therefore rejoice, O heavens, and you who dwell in them!* Woe to the inhabitants of the earth and the sea [unregenerate, unrepentant sinners]! For the devil has come down to you, having great wrath, because he knows that he has a short time. Now when the dragon saw that he had been cast to the earth, he persecuted the woman who gave birth to the male Child [the church]. But the woman was given *two wings of a great eagle* [the apostolic and prophetic anointing], that she might fly into the wilderness to her place, where

she is nourished for a time and times and half a time [three and one half years], from the presence of the serpent. So the serpent spewed water out of his mouth like a flood [of persecution] after the woman, that he might cause her to be carried away by the flood. But the earth helped the woman, and the earth opened its mouth and swallowed up the flood which the dragon had spewed out of his mouth. And the dragon was enraged with the woman, and he went to make war with the rest of her offspring, who keep the commandments of God and have the testimony of Jesus Christ. (Rev. 12:11–17; italics mine)

After the defeat of Satan, the angel who spoke to John said, "Therefore rejoice, O heavens, and you who dwell in them!" In the midst of all the world's fear and calamity, the saints are instructed to rejoice! They have hope that the world doesn't have. They have numerous reasons to rejoice:

Arise, shine; For your light has come! And the glory of the LORD is risen upon you. For behold, the darkness shall cover the earth, And deep darkness the people; *But the LORD will arise over you, And His glory will be seen upon you.* The Gentiles shall come to your light, And kings to the brightness of your rising. Lift up your eyes all around, and see: They all gather together, they come to you; *Your sons shall come from afar, And your daughters shall be nursed at your side.* Then you shall see and become radiant, And your heart shall swell with joy; Because the *abundance* of the sea shall be turned to you, The *wealth* of the Gentiles shall come to you. (Isa. 60:1–5; italics mine)

Why rejoice? One of the most important reasons is the prodigals are coming home! "Your sons shall come from afar, And your daughters shall be nursed at your side. Then you shall see and become radiant, And your heart shall swell with joy; Because *the abundance of the sea shall be turned to you*." There is an abundant harvest of souls coming in. The *sea* is symbolic for the world's population, and being turned (or converted, as the KJV translates it) is God bringing in the great, end-time harvest of souls, including our own children!

Besides rejoicing over His promise to save our children, on January 1, 2017, the Lord spoke to me and said, "Tell my people to ask for everything they have lost, had stolen from them or that they have been deprived of, and I will restore it to them because this is the beginning of the days of the restoration of all things spoken by the prophets from the beginning of creation" (see Acts 3:21).

Of course the primary things that we should ask for are the precious spiritual things that the early church had but gradually lost over time, such as tremendous miracle working power accompanied with many signs and wonders. But God's promise to restore all things isn't limited to spiritual things. Isaiah said, "The wealth of the Gentiles shall come to you." Although this includes wealth coming to the Israelites, it isn't limited to them. Solomon said, "A good man leaves an inheritance to his children's children, But the wealth of the sinner is stored up for the righteous" (Prov. 13:22). God is going to finance the end-time harvest with the spoils of war! He has a transfer of wealth from the wicked to the righteous on His agenda!

After Job successfully overcame Satan's tremendous onslaught against him, in which he lost everything, God mercifully restored everything back to him, double (except for his children), so that in the end he had twice as much as he started with (see Job 1:3, 42:12). There's nothing impossible for God. He will either restore everything as it was before or replace it with something better (2 Cor. 1:7).

Joel also gives us an insight into God's gracious restoration plan that is relevant to the time of the "latter rain" in which we live:

> Be glad then, you children of Zion, And
> rejoice in the Lord your God; For He has given

you the former rain faithfully, And He will cause the rain to come down for you—*The former rain, And the latter rain in the first month.* The threshing floors shall be full of wheat, And the vats shall overflow with new wine and oil. *So I will restore to you the years that the swarming locust has eaten, The crawling locust, The consuming locust, And the chewing locust, My great army which I sent among you.* You shall eat in plenty and be satisfied, And praise the name of the Lord your God, Who has dealt wondrously with you; And My people shall never be put to shame. (Joel 2:23–26; italics mine)

Now we need to interpret a prophecy from Isaiah that parallels the opening of the sixth seal. Isaiah's progressive, end-time vision covers a period of time that has already lasted over one hundred years. We briefly examined a portion of it in chapter 5:

There will be on every high mountain And on every high hill Rivers and streams of waters, In the day of the great slaughter, When the towers fall. Moreover the light of the moon will be as the light of the sun, And the light of the sun will be sevenfold, As the light of seven days, In the day that the Lord binds up the bruise of His people And heals the stroke of their wound. Behold, the name of the Lord comes from afar, Burning with His anger, And His burden is heavy; His lips are full of indignation, And His tongue like a devouring fire. His breath is like an overflowing stream, Which reaches up to the neck, To sift the nations with the sieve of futility; And there shall be a bridle in the jaws of the people, Causing them to err. (Isa. 30:25–28)

We previously interpreted the rivers and streams of waters as the outpouring of the Holy Spirit that began in 1906 and the spiritual reformation that followed. This second reformation began the process of bringing in the great end-time harvest, as Isaiah prophesied:

> For I will pour water upon him that is thirsty, and floods upon the dry ground: I will pour my spirit upon thy seed, and my blessing upon thine offspring. (Isa. 44:3)

Then, in 1948, after the restoration of Israel as a nation, a second wave of spiritual renewal was birthed. This wave was originally called the *latter rain*. This worldwide revival quickly morphed into the charismatic movement, which lasted about fifty years. Now it is time for the rest of Joel's prophetic promise to be fulfilled:

> For He has given you the former rain faithfully, And He will cause the rain to come down for you—*the former rain, and the latter rain in the first month*. The threshing floors shall be full of wheat, And the vats shall overflow with new wine and oil. (Joel 2:23–24; italics mine)

There is a *third* wave, consisting of both the early and latter rain being poured out together! *There is a tsunami coming!* Isaiah associated its appearance with the fall of the twin towers (9/11/2001), so the church should be preparing itself to receive a spiritual deluge!

Earlier we interpreted the moon as the church and the sun as God in Christ, the light of the world, but Isaiah prophesied that in the latter days, His light will shine brighter than ever before. The light of the sun being sevenfold means a complete revelation of all things hidden. As Jesus promised the disciples, every hidden mystery is being unsealed and revealed at this time (see Matthew 13:11). Therefore, Isaiah is saying that as darkness falls upon the world, the church will arise and shine with the full brilliance and glory of the Son of God! He also prophesied of the restoration and salvation of

Israel (which we will discuss later). The latter part of his vision foretells the deception that is coming upon the whole world and the outpouring of God's fiery wrath upon the ungodly.

Jesus promised, "He that believeth on me, the works that I do shall he do also; and greater works than these shall he do; because I go unto my Father" (John 14:12). As we saw in Job's case, God restores double. Elisha, operating under the anointing of Elijah, performed twice as many miracles as Elijah did—so through Christ's resurrection power and anointing, we will do even greater works than He did:

> Return to the stronghold, You prisoners of hope. Even today I declare That I will restore double to you. (Zech. 9:12)
>
> Instead of your shame you shall have double honor, And instead of confusion they shall rejoice in their portion. Therefore in their land they shall possess double; Everlasting joy shall be theirs. (Isa. 61:7)

From these scriptures, and many like them, we can see that although gross "darkness shall cover the earth," God's people have every reason to rejoice (see Isaiah 60:1–2).

And finally, although it isn't something to rejoice over, Isaiah prophesied that "there shall be a bridle in the jaws of the people, Causing them to err." This is in reference to the great deception that God will send to test the sincerity of the saints' love for Him. This lie will deceive many because they do not love the truth. We will discuss this great deception in chapter 11:

> For the mystery of lawlessness is already at work; only He who now restrains will do so until He is taken out of the way. And then the lawless one will be revealed, whom the Lord will consume with the breath of His mouth and destroy with the brightness of His coming. The coming

of the lawless one is according to the working of Satan, with all power, signs, and lying wonders, and with all unrighteous deception among those who perish, *because they did not receive the love of the truth*, that they might be saved. And *for this reason God will send them strong delusion, that they should believe the lie*, that they all may be condemned who did not believe the truth but had pleasure in unrighteousness. (2 Thess. 2:7–12; italics mine)

Chapter 9

The Lord's Army

Before any nation deliberately goes to war, they raise, equip, and train an army in preparation for the coming conflict. Since nothing catches God by surprise, when war breaks out in heaven, He is well prepared.

> After these things I saw *four angels* standing at the four corners of the earth, holding the four winds of the earth, that the wind should not blow on the earth, on the sea, or on any tree. Then I saw another angel ascending from the east, having the seal of the living God. And he cried with a loud voice to the four angels to whom it was granted to harm the earth and the sea, saying, "*Do not harm the earth, the sea, or the trees till we have sealed the servants of our God on their foreheads.*" (Rev. 7:1–3; italics mine)

This juncture in Revelation's time line (the waiting period that exists between the sixth and seventh seal) is where we are at this present time. God has stopped the forward advancement of time until He has gathered in the final harvest of souls. This time of waiting corresponds to God waiting for Noah to build the ark and gather in the animals before He sent the rain (see 1 Peter 3:20). The four angels who are withheld from harming the earth will be loosed as soon as the harvest is over. They are the first four of the seven who administer the great tribulation (the last three release the *three woes* upon the earth—which we will discuss in chapter 12). The army chosen below is actually an army of harvesters (see Luke 10:2):

> And I heard the number of those who were sealed. *One hundred and forty-four thousand* of all the tribes of the children of Israel were sealed: of the tribe of Judah [He shall be praised] twelve thousand were sealed; of the tribe of Reuben [see, a son] twelve thousand were sealed; of the tribe of Gad [a troop or invader] twelve thousand were sealed; of the tribe of Asher [happy] twelve thousand were sealed; of the tribe of Naphtali [my wrestling] twelve thousand were sealed; of the tribe of Manasseh [causing to forget] twelve thousand were sealed; of the tribe of Simeon [harkening] twelve thousand were sealed; of the tribe of Levi [joined] twelve thousand were sealed; of the tribe of Issachar [he will be hired or there is a reward] twelve thousand were sealed; of the tribe of Zebulun [dwelling] twelve thousand were sealed; of the tribe of Joseph [let him aid or add Jehovah] twelve thousand were sealed; of the tribe of Benjamin [son of the right hand] twelve thousand were sealed. (Rev. 7:1–8; italics mine)

In Revelation, some names and numbers are literal, and some are symbolic. The context, alone, determines which way they are being used in any given passage. Close examination reveals that both the names and numbers of the tribes in this army are symbolic—both Dan and Ephraim are missing, and Joseph and Levi are put in their place—but Joseph isn't a tribe, and Levi isn't counted as one because he didn't receive an inheritance in Israel. The Lord was his inheritance (see Numbers 1:47–49).

When Joshua led Israel into Canaan and conquered the seven nations who occupied it, he divided the land among the twelve tribes as an inheritance. Each tribe received a section that may be compared to one of our states, here in the USA.

Of Jacob's twelve sons, Joseph, received the right of the firstborn because Reuben, Jacob's firstborn son, sinned against Jacob. Therefore, the right of the firstborn passed to Joseph, Jacob's second wife's firstborn. So Joseph received a double portion through his two sons, Ephraim and Manasseh. Each son became a separate tribe. Although Ephraim became the largest of all the ten northern tribes, his name isn't listed in this army.

So this army is a parable. It should be considered symbolic because it cannot be literal. As we unseal each of its symbols, keep in mind that this is God's army. Its twofold purpose is to gather in the end-time harvest of souls and in the process bring those who reject the gospel message and refuse to repent of their ungodly deeds into full accountability for their sins.

When Moses assembled the twelve tribes, he stationed them in four groups of three tribes each. As always, Judah goes first. His name means "he shall be praised." Reuben means "see, a son," and Gad means "a troop"—so this army's first division reveals that *this troop of warrior sons will bring praise and glory to God.*

Asher means "happy," Naphtali means "my wrestling," and Manasseh means "causing to forget." The hidden message of this division is *their wrestling will prevail and annihilate the forces of evil and bring joy to the saints, because the former things are forgotten and the past is remembered no more.*

Simeon means "harkening," Levi means "joined," and Issachar means "there is a reward." The message here is this: *God is assuring all who join with Christ and wage war with Him that they will be amply rewarded for their service, suffering, and sacrifice* (see Matthew 19:29).

And last of all, Zebulun means "dwelling," Joseph means "let him aid" or "add Jehovah," and Benjamin means "son of the right hand." This last division is summed up by what Paul said in

Ephesians 2:22, that *the sons of God, who are Christ's body, are "being built together for a dwelling place of God in the Spirit."*

In the first chapter, we disclosed that the things that John saw in heaven have their counterpart here on earth. This army of one hundred and forty-four thousand actually represents the end-time, remnant church. It consists of everyone of God's faithful warriors who are *sealed with the Holy Spirit of promise* (see Ephesians 1:13; 6:10–18).

In John's vision, the number of each tribe is also symbolic. Each tribe is composed of twelve thousand men. Twelve signifies they are *united*, and thousand means they are *mature*, so these mature troops are *of one mind and one accord*. Likewise, one means "beginning"; hundred means "full or fulness"; four means "rule or dominion"; and forty means "rule that has been tried and tested (and in this case), approved and accepted." Therefore, this army of one hundred and forty-four thousand firstborn sons is *a mature, fully trained army, who are well equipped (with the sword of the Spirit) to exercise dominion over their enemies!*

Is the church army actually limited to 144,000? No, not at all! The number is symbolic. This question is like asking if the moon is actually going to be turned into blood or if the sun is going to get seven times hotter! Of course they aren't (see Acts 2:20; Isaiah 30:26). Once a symbol is interpreted, the meaning should be kept, and the symbol itself should be discarded. To retain the symbol in the interpretation is like removing the husk that covers wheat kernels and then mixing them back into the flour before making bread. These symbols are like many others used in Scripture. Those who wait and look for a natural manifestation often fail to recognize the actual fulfillment when it appears.

God's army is comparable to,

> The sons of Reuben, the Gadites, and half the tribe of Manasseh [who] had forty-four thousand seven hundred and sixty valiant men, *men able to bear shield and sword, to shoot with the bow,*

and skillful in war, who went to war. (1 Chron. 5:18; italics mine)

These ancient warriors used natural weapons—God's end-time army uses spiritual weapons that are "mighty in God for pulling down strongholds" (see 2 Corinthians 10:3–4).

Although God's end-time, volunteer army has more than one purpose, one of its more important purposes is to make the world fully accountable for its sins. This is accomplished by bearing witness to the resurrection of Jesus Christ by the demonstration of God's miraculous power. We will discuss this in chapter 11.

Chapter 10

Revelation's Time Line

The fourteenth chapter of Revelation reveals a sequence of events, in chronological order, that transpire during the end-times. Each event is announced by a different angel. In this chapter, we will examine a brief overview of John's time line, then in the following chapters, we will give an in-depth discussion of each event in the sequence that it unfolds:

God's Army

In this section of John's first vision, which we discussed in the preceding chapter, he saw an army of saints who were redeemed and equipped for war. They were standing on Mount Zion, which is the church, so this army is actually composed of members of the end-time church:

> Then I looked, and behold, a Lamb standing on Mount Zion [which is the church, see Hebrews 12:22–24], and with Him [an army consisting of] one hundred and forty-four thousand, having His Father's name written on their foreheads. And I heard a voice from heaven, like the voice of many waters, and like the voice of

loud thunder. And I heard the sound of harpists playing their harps. They sang as it were a new song before the throne, before the four living creatures, and the elders; and no one could learn that song except the hundred and forty-four thousand who were redeemed from the earth. (Rev. 14:1–3)

These are not resurrected saints who are in the third heaven (the paradise of God) but rather faithful saints "who love not their lives unto death" who are victorious as they war in the second heaven. The song they sing is a song of victory!

Many have thought this passage of scripture was speaking of the rapture because they are called "firstfruits," but Paul uses that term for those who have the Holy Spirit (see Romans 8:23), and James calls those who are saved firstfruits. *Firstfruits* refer to those saints who will be in the first resurrection versus the harvest of souls that will be saved during the millennial reign of Christ:

> Of His own will He brought us forth by the word of truth, that we might be a kind of firstfruits of His creatures. (Jas. 1:18)

The Gospel of the Kingdom

The first angel John saw announces the preaching of the gospel to the whole world, which Jesus said must take place before the end will come:

> And this gospel of the kingdom will be preached in all the world as a witness to all the nations, and then the end will come. (Matt. 24:14)

John said this flying angel carried *the everlasting gospel*, which is for every nation on earth, announcing the hour of God's judgment:

> Then I saw another angel flying in the midst of heaven, having the everlasting gospel to preach to those who dwell on the earth—to every nation, tribe, tongue, and people—saying with a loud voice, *"Fear God and give glory to Him, for the hour of His judgment has come*; and worship Him who made heaven and earth, the sea and springs of water." (Rev. 14:6–7; italics mine)

We are presently at this juncture in Revelation's time line. This time corresponds to the battle where Joshua stopped the sun and moon until the five kings of the Philistines were defeated. Everything is on hold until the Lord's enemies are made His footstool (see Joshua 10:12–13; Psalm 110:1–3). As you can see from this angel's announcement of the coming judgment, the beginning of John's time line discussed in this chapter parallels the opening of the sixth seal, which we discussed in chapter 5.

The Great Tribulation

After the Gentile harvest is complete, the world enters into a time of testing and turmoil the likes of which it has never experienced since the beginning of time. During this time, a beast arises who, using guile and diplomacy, successfully gains power and authority over the whole world. At the same time, two wicked parasites, Jezebel and the Antichrist, struggle to take advantage of his rise to power to gain world supremacy for themselves.

The First Beast

Once the full gospel message has been preached throughout the whole world with confirming signs and wonders, Satan arises in one final, desperate attempt to take over the world and annihilate the church:

> Then I stood on the sand of the sea. And I saw a beast rising up out of the sea, having seven heads and ten horns, and on his horns ten crowns… The dragon [Satan] gave him his power, his throne, and great authority. And I saw one of his heads as if it had been mortally wounded, and his deadly wound was healed. And all the world marveled and followed the beast. So they worshiped the dragon who gave authority to the beast; and they worshiped the beast, saying, "Who is like the beast? Who is able to make war with him?" (Rev. 13:1–4)

Mystery Babylon's Fall

When this beast arises from the sea, Jezebel is sitting on his back (see Revelation 17:3; we will discuss this strange partnership in chapter 14). After he successfully gains power over the whole world, an angel appears announcing God's judgment being executed upon Babylon. Babylon, alias Jezebel, is called *Mystery Babylon* in Revelation 17:5, to distinguish her from the natural city and kingdom of Babylon. There is a natural Jerusalem and a new Jerusalem. The first is natural, the second spiritual. Likewise, there is a natural Babylon and Mystery Babylon—the first natural and the second spiritual. It is important to distinguish this difference when interpreting Scripture:

> And another angel followed, saying, "[Mystery] Babylon is fallen, is fallen, that great city, because she has made all nations drink of the wine of the wrath of her fornication." (Rev. 14:8)

The Antichrist

The swift, diplomatic takeover of all nations by the first beast opens the way for the long anticipated appearing of the Antichrist. It is important to note that John also called the Antichrist a false prophet. The title, "the false prophet," is in reference to his close association with, and exaltation of, the first beast:

> Then I saw another beast coming up out of the earth, and he had two horns like a lamb and spoke like a dragon. And he exercises all the authority of the first beast in his presence, and *causes the earth and those who dwell in it to worship the first beast*, whose deadly wound was healed. (Rev. 13:11–12; italics mine)

The third angel John saw announces the revealing of the Antichrist and warns of the dire consequences of worshipping him and taking his mark. The sequence of these events allows us to place his appearing as being either synonymous with or immediately after the initial fall of Babylon (see 2 Thessalonians 2:3–8):

> Then a third angel followed them, saying with a loud voice, "If anyone worships the beast and his image, and receives his mark on his forehead or on his hand, he himself shall also drink of the wine of the wrath of God, which is poured out full strength into the cup of His indignation. He shall be tormented with fire and brimstone in the presence of the holy angels and in the presence of the Lamb. And the smoke of their torment ascends forever and ever; and they have no rest day or night, who worship the beast and his image, and whoever receives the mark of his name." (Rev. 14:9–11)

The Persecution of the Saints

Then in the following two verses, John refers to the time of testing and persecution that we previously discussed in chapter 4, when the fifth and sixth seals were opened. During this time, the saints are refined and purified through the ordeals of persecution:

> Here is the patience of the saints; here are those who keep the commandments of God and the faith of Jesus. Then I heard a voice from heaven saying to me, "Write: Blessed are the dead who die in the Lord from now on." "Yes," says the Spirit, "that they may rest from their labors, and their works follow them." (Rev. 14:12–13)

Just how severe the persecution will be is revealed in Revelation, chapter 12. This passage of scripture has been misinterpreted for decades, if not for centuries:

> And another sign appeared in heaven: behold, a great, *fiery red* dragon having seven heads and ten horns, and seven diadems on his heads. *His tail drew a third of the stars of heaven and threw them to the earth.* And the dragon stood before the woman who was ready to give birth, to devour her Child as soon as it was born. (Rev. 12:3–4; italics mine)

John's description of the fiery red dragon with seven heads, whose tail drew a third of the stars down and cast them to the earth, has been interpreted as Satan's original fall in the garden of Eden. It is taught that one-third of the angels followed him, leaving God with two-thirds. As we discussed in chapter 7, the problem with that interpretation is that John was told to "write the things which you have seen, and the things which are, and the things which will take place after this" (Rev. 1:1), and the original fall of Satan was thousands of years before John's time. You cannot legitimately take the twelfth chapter of Revelation and place it back in Genesis!

The stars that John saw the dragon's tail pull down are saints. The seven-headed, fiery red dragon is Satan working in and through the first beast. (*Fiery red*, as in the fiery red horse in the second seal, indicates persecution). His tail is the Antichrist, whom John identifies as "the false prophet" (see below). Isaiah interpreted the tail as the false prophet, and Daniel prophesied the saint's fall:

> Then the [first] beast was captured, and with him *the false prophet* [the Antichrist] who worked signs in his presence, by which he deceived those who received the mark of the beast and those who worshiped his image. These two were cast alive into the lake of fire burning with brimstone. (Rev. 19:20; italics mine)

> The [false] prophet who teaches lies, he is the tail. (Isa. 9:15)

> And some [one-third] of those of understanding shall fall, to refine them, purify them, and make them white, until the time of the end; because it is still for the appointed time. (Dan. 11:35)

Why is the Antichrist considered a *false prophet?* Because *a prophet is one who speaks the word and does the work of another*, and the Antichrist promotes the first beast's image and mark rather than his own. Although he claims to be exalting the first beast, his conduct shows that in reality, everything he does is for his own fame and gain. Paul said the

> man of sin…opposes and exalts himself above all that is called God or that is worshiped, so that he sits as God in the temple of God, showing himself that he is God [and] The coming of

the lawless one is according to the working of
Satan, with all power, signs, and lying wonders.
(2 Thess. 2:3–4, 9)

As we saw in the first chapter, when we misinterpret a symbol, we misunderstand and misapply the message it conveys. The falling stars represent one-third of the saints being persecuted. So obviously, it isn't the rapture that is next on the church's agenda that we should be getting prepared for; it is severe persecution, which comes *before* the rapture!

The Rapture

After this, John saw the rapture, which is the first resurrection. Since the events announced by the angels in Revelation, chapter 14, are sequential, this is one of several confirmations that many of the saints will have to endure the tribulation and resist the temptation to take the mark of the beast before being caught up into the air to be with Christ:

> Then I looked, and behold, a white cloud, and on the cloud sat One like the Son of Man, having on His head a golden crown, and in His hand a sharp sickle. And another angel came out of the temple, crying with a loud voice to Him who sat on the cloud, "Thrust in Your sickle and reap, for the time has come for You to reap, for the harvest of the earth is ripe." So He who sat on the cloud thrust in His sickle on the earth, and the earth was reaped. (Rev. 14:14–16)

This harvest which is conducted by the "Son of Man" is the fulfillment of James 5:7, "Therefore be patient, brethren, until the coming of the Lord. See how the farmer waits for the precious fruit of the earth, waiting patiently for it until it receives the early and latter rain." The early rain fell at Pentecost. The latter rain, which ripens the fruit harvest, is the outpouring of the Spirit which is taking place now. As we have seen, soon, both the early and latter rain will be poured out together, releasing an unprecedented revelation of God's power and glory upon the earth.

The Great Day of His Wrath

After this final, end-time harvest of souls is complete and the rapture takes place, John saw the righteous judgment of God's fiery wrath being poured out upon the unrepentant sinners in the earth!

> Then another angel came out of the temple which is in heaven, he also having a sharp sickle. And another angel came out from the altar, who had power over fire, and he cried with a loud cry to him who had the sharp sickle, saying, "Thrust in your sharp sickle and gather the clusters of the vine of the earth, for her grapes are fully ripe." So the angel thrust his sickle into the earth and gathered the vine of the earth, and threw it into the great winepress of the wrath of God. And the winepress was trampled outside the city, and blood came out of the winepress, up to the horses' bridles, for one thousand six hundred furlongs. [about two hundred miles!] (Rev. 14:17–20.)

Chapter 11

Revelation's Time Line Expanded

In the last chapter, we gave a brief overview of Revelation's time line, showing the sequence of specific events that make up the end-times. Now we need to expound upon each of these events, individually.

The fourteenth chapter of Revelation opens with the introduction of God's unique, Holy Spirit–sealed army, indicating that from this point on, during the unfolding of time, there is war—both natural and spiritual warfare—but war, nevertheless. The war that started on the home front, where the saints overcame the dragon (Satan) and cast him out of the second heaven, now continues in the earth. But before the curtain can close on the dispensation of grace and usher in the millennial age, the gospel of the kingdom must first be preached to all the world.

THE THREE WITNESSES

> Then I saw another angel flying in the midst of heaven, having *the everlasting gospel* to preach to those who dwell on the earth—to every nation, tribe, tongue, and people—saying with a

loud voice, "*Fear God and give glory to Him, for the hour of His judgment has come*; and worship Him who made heaven and earth, the sea and springs of water." (Rev. 14:6–7; italics mine)

It is important to note that the angel emphasized that the "hour of His judgment has come"! This end-time kingdom message isn't just about the mercy of the Lamb; instead, it contains a distinct warning of the approaching wrath ministered by the Lion of Judah. The modern, Laodicean church's overemphasis on God's love and mercy has all but erased the fear of God in the church. The "severity of God" is as real as His mercy!

Therefore *consider the goodness and severity of God: on those who fell, severity*; but toward you, goodness, if you continue in His goodness. Otherwise you also will be cut off. (Rom. 11:22; italics mine; also see Psalm 11:5–6)

Although the gospel has been preached for centuries, it takes more than just preaching the word to bring the world into accountability. Paul said,

And my speech and my preaching were not with persuasive words of human wisdom, but in demonstration of the Spirit and of power, that your faith should not be in the wisdom of men but in the power of God. (1 Cor. 2:4–5)

God desires to give the world three witnesses that testify of the resurrection of Jesus Christ—the word, the Spirit, and the Father's works (miracles—see Acts 4:33; John 10:37–38). At Jesus' next appearing, He will scorch the earth with fire! Isaiah said that God "will make a mortal more rare than fine gold" (Isa. 13:12). When He returns, billions of sinners will be executed by the fires of His wrath, so He is restrained by His own word from appearing until the world has had sufficient witness to be fully accountable:

> Whoever is deserving of death shall be put to death on the testimony of two or three witnesses; he shall not be put to death on the testimony of one witness. (Deut. 17:6)

Concerning the concept of more than one witness being required before anyone can be held accountable and justice rendered, Jesus said,

> If I had not come and spoken to them, they would have no sin, but now they have no excuse for their sin. He who hates Me hates My Father also. If I had not done among them the works which no one else did, they would have no sin; but *now they have seen and also hated both Me and My Father*. (John 15:22–24; italics mine)

The Completion of Christ's Ministry

When Jesus came the first time, He only ministered three and one-half years. Seven is the number of completion, so, obviously, His ministry is incomplete. The last three and one-half years of His ministry will be performed by and through the church. In the same way that Paul labored with spiritual birth pains for Christ to be manifested in and through the Galatians, John saw the end-time church laboring in travail for Christ to be manifested in and through them as a final witness to the whole world:

> My little children, for whom I labor in birth again until Christ is formed in you. (Gal. 4:19)
>
> Now a great sign appeared in heaven: a woman clothed with the sun, with the moon under her feet, and on her head a garland of

> twelve stars. Then being with child, she cried out in labor and in pain to give birth. (Rev. 12:1–2)

This woman is the remnant church. A garland was a wreathe awarded to the Olympic game winners; thus the garland of twelve stars depicts a victorious, fully apostolic church. Being clothed with the sun signifies the Holy Spirit anointing, and the moon under her feet shows that she is an overcomer (see Romans 8:35–37). As we discussed in chapter 8, at this point in time, "the light of the moon will be as the light of the sun, And the light of the sun will be sevenfold, As the light of seven days" (Isa. 30:26).

Although it is a progressive illumination, the church will shine with the full brilliance of the Son of God before Christ's ministry to the world is complete. ("But the path of the just is like the shining sun, That shines ever brighter unto the perfect day" [Prov. 4:18]). It is during this second half of Jesus' ministry that the *judicial* aspect of His ministry will be manifested. Isaiah prophesied that Christ came "To proclaim the acceptable year of the Lord, *And the day of vengeance of our God*; To comfort all who mourn" (Isa. 61:2; italics mine).

What does the judicial aspect of Christ's ministry look like? The gospel is good news for the righteous, but not so for the ungodly! The twenty-first century church has over-emphasized God's love and mercy to the point that the fear of God no longer exists in the church or in society. Although Paul said the goodness of God leads to repentance, when necessary, His goodness includes executing severe judgments and administering painful chastisements upon disobedient sinners (see Romans 2:4–9; Hebrews 12:5–11; Acts 5:1–11). Isaiah said,

> With my soul I have desired You in the night, Yes, by my spirit within me I will seek You early; For when Your judgments are in the earth, The inhabitants of the world will learn righteousness. *Let grace be shown to the wicked, Yet he will not learn righteousness; In the land of uprightness he*

> *will deal unjustly, And will not behold the majesty of the* Lord. (Isa. 26:9–10; italics mine)

We are not doing an ungodly person a favor by continually telling him that God loves him and offering him mercy, when God is actually completely fed up with his wickedness—and God's patience *can* be exhausted!

> He who is often rebuked, and hardens his neck, Will suddenly be destroyed, and that without remedy. (Prov. 29:1)

Although God is long-suffering and *willing* to love everyone, if they will repent and change their ways, He explicitly said that there are those whom His soul hates (see Psalm 5:5; Romans 9:13):

> The Lord tests the righteous, *But the wicked and the one who loves violence His soul hates.* Upon the wicked He will rain coals; Fire and brimstone and a burning wind Shall be the portion of their cup. (Ps. 11:5–6; italics mine)

The full, powerful manifestation of the judicial aspects of Christ's ministry will be short-lived. After three and one-half years, the night will fall. Jesus said, "I must work the works of Him who sent Me while it is day; the night is coming when no one can work" (John 9:4). Satan threw everything he had at Jesus to cut Him off the first time that He came, and he has more in his arsenal to fight with this time than he did then.

> And another sign appeared in heaven: behold, a great, fiery red dragon having seven heads and ten horns, and seven diadems on his heads. His tail drew a third of the stars of heaven and threw them to the earth. And the dragon stood before the woman who was ready to give

> birth, to devour her Child as soon as it was born. She bore a male Child who was to rule all nations with a rod of iron. And her Child was caught up to God and His throne. (Rev. 12:3–5)

Satan will launch a preemptive attack in an attempt to abort Christ's full manifestation and ministry through the church. Although he will incite worldwide persecution against the church, that will eventually encompass one-third of the saints, ultimately, he will fail.

Although the fullness of Christ's ministry will be short, as we saw above, the light will shine so bright that it will reveal the burning hatred the world has for its creator. Jesus prophesied of these times. "Then they will deliver you up to tribulation and kill you, and you will be hated by all nations for My name's sake" (Matt. 24:9). From this point on, Satan has no mediator in the church and is completely cast out:

> Now when the dragon saw that he had been cast to the earth, he persecuted the woman who gave birth to the male Child. *But the woman was given two wings of a great eagle, that she might fly into the wilderness to her place, where she is nourished for a time and times and half a time, from the presence of the serpent.* So the serpent spewed water out of his mouth like a flood after the woman, that he might cause her to be carried away by the flood. *But the earth helped the woman, and the earth opened its mouth and swallowed up the flood which the dragon had spewed out of his mouth.* And the dragon was enraged with the woman, and he went to make war with the rest of her offspring, who keep the commandments of God and have the testimony of Jesus Christ. (Rev. 12:13–17; italics mine)

The Seventh Seal

Once Jesus' three-and-one-half-year ministry is complete and the fullness of the Gentile harvest has been gathered in, the seventh seal will be opened, and heaven will become silent for about half an hour:

> When He opened the seventh seal, there was silence in heaven for about half an hour. (Rev. 8:1)

"About half an hour" will probably be about three and one-half years. During this time of silence, the powerful manifestation of Christ's Spirit and presence will be withdrawn. John said that He would be "caught up to God and His throne," thus allowing the Antichrist to reveal himself. Paul said, "For the mystery of lawlessness is already at work; only He [Christ] who now restrains will do so until He is taken out of the way" (2 Thess. 2:7). Jesus gave us a veiled hint of this when He was talking with the disciples. He said, "I will no longer talk much with you, *for the ruler of this world is coming*, and he has nothing in Me" (John 14:30; italics mine).

The fact that He was speaking prophetically is revealed in that nothing in His conduct changed at that time. He kept right on teaching and training them as before. Also, at that time, Judas was the one who was coming, not the "ruler of this world" (the first beast followed by the Antichrist).

There is no scriptural explanation as to how the earth will swallow up the flood of persecution and help the woman, but one possibility is this—the God initiated persecution of Jezebel by the ten kings, which begins around this time, will take precedence over the Antichrist's vicious attempts to annihilate the saints and distract him from his evil purpose (see Revelation 17:16–17).

Once the latter half of Christ's ministry is complete and heaven becomes silent, God's promise to the Philadelphia church will come to fruition, and *the remnant church* will be hidden:

> Because you have kept My command to persevere, I also will keep you from the hour of trial which shall come upon the whole world, to test those who dwell on the earth. (Rev. 3:10)

But beware! Jesus implied that not everyone who calls himself a Christian will be counted worthy to be shielded in this way:

> But take heed to yourselves, lest your hearts be weighed down with carousing, drunkenness, and cares of this life, and that Day come on you unexpectedly. For it will come as a snare on all those who dwell on the face of the whole earth. *Watch therefore, and pray always that you may be counted worthy to escape all these things that will come to pass*, and to stand before the Son of Man. (Luke 21:34–36; italics mine)

The saints who *do* qualify have a promise of divine protection, which John says will last just seventeen days short of three and one-half years (which explains the "about" half an hour of silence):

> Then the woman fled into the wilderness, where she has a place prepared by God, that they should feed her there one thousand two hundred and sixty days. (Rev. 12:6)

> He who dwells in the secret place of the Most High Shall abide under the shadow of the Almighty. I will say of the Lord, "He is my refuge and my fortress; My God, in Him I will trust." …A thousand may fall at your side, And ten thousand at your right hand; But it shall not come near you. Only with your eyes shall you look, And see the reward of the wicked. Because you have made the Lord, who is my refuge, Even

the Most High, your dwelling place, No evil shall befall you, Nor shall any plague come near your dwelling; For He shall give His angels charge over you, To keep you in all your ways. (Ps. 91:1–3, 7–11)

How and where this concealment takes place, no one knows (if we knew, so would Satan), but perhaps it will be similar to those Obadiah hid during Jezebel's persecution of the prophets in Elijah's day. Also, during that time, God hid Elijah from Ahab until He was ready for him to confront Israel on Mount Carmel (which corresponds to the two witnesses' ministry to Israel, which we will discuss in chapter 12—see 1 Kings 18:1–39).

Until the whole world has been given all three witnesses—the Son's *word*, the Holy Spirit's *manifestations,* and the Father's *miraculous works*—Jesus will not return. But the most eye-opening and startling truth contained in Revelation is the fact that once the church completes its commission to bear witness of the resurrection of Christ to the whole world, *everything from that point to the rapture takes place within as little as seven to ten years!* Paul said, "For He will finish the work and cut it short in righteousness, Because the Lord will make a short work upon the earth" (Romans 9:28).

Following the completion of Christ's ministry through the church, which brings the whole world into accountability, Mystery Babylon is judged and God's righteous judgments are executed upon her—and not her only—but all those who are deceived by her. But before this can take place, the final power struggle between God and Satan for control over the whole world takes place.

The Great Tribulation

Although we will discuss the seven trumpets that administer the great tribulation in detail in the next chapter, I've included it here to establish the timing of its commencement.

The First Beast

In the strange world of spiritual warfare, when it is time for God to act, Satan reacts, often preemptively (as when he tried to kill Moses before he could grow up and deliver Israel from Egyptian bondage. This is also the primary reason he has incited worldwide abortion, to hinder God from raising up the end-time army we discussed in chapter 9). Once God has brought the world into full accountability by the preaching of the gospel of the kingdom, Satan makes one last, desperate attempt to gain the upper hand and extend his time here on the earth:

> Then I stood on the sand of the sea. And I saw a beast rising up out of the sea, having seven heads and ten horns, and on his horns ten crowns... The dragon [Satan] gave him his power, his throne, and great authority. And I saw one of his heads as if it had been mortally wounded, and his deadly wound was healed. And all the world marveled and followed the beast. So they worshiped the dragon who gave authority to the beast; and they worshiped the beast, saying, "Who is like the beast? Who is able to make war with him?" And he was given a mouth speaking great things and blasphemies, and *he was given authority to continue for forty-two months*. Then he opened his mouth in blasphemy against God, to blaspheme His name, His tabernacle, and those who dwell in heaven. It was granted to him to make war with the saints and to overcome them. And authority was given him over every tribe, tongue, and nation. All who dwell on the earth will worship him, whose names have not been written in the Book of Life of the Lamb slain from the foundation of the world. (Rev. 13:1–8; italics mine)

Apparently, in the beast's struggle for world supremacy, one of his confederate nations is given a fatal blow in war (see Revelation 13:14). Nevertheless, it miraculously recovers, which causes all nations to perceive the beast as invincible. We will discuss this first satanic beast in greater detail in chapter 14.

Mystery Babylon's Judgment

> And another angel followed, saying, "Babylon is fallen, is fallen, that great city, because she has made all nations drink of the wine of the wrath of her fornication." (Rev. 14:8)

The Babylon referred to here is Mystery Babylon, not the literal city. In His letter to Thyatira, Christ promised to "cast [Jezebel] into a sickbed, and those who commit adultery with her into great tribulation" (Rev. 2:20). Jezebel and Mystery Babylon are synonymous. They are one and the same. The angel told John, "And the woman [Jezebel] whom you saw is that great city which reigns over the kings of the earth" (Rev. 17:18).

Both symbols portray the powerful, deceitful religious system that has replaced God's word with "the writings of the Fathers," Christ with church tradition, and the Holy Spirit with religious rituals. Many will "commit adultery" with the harlot. She is going to make many enticing offers in the days ahead, whereby many will be deceived.

Babylon's judgment is executed in two stages. First, she will be severely persecuted by the ten kings during the latter half of the great tribulation, then completely destroyed when the bowls of God's wrath are poured out upon the earth (much more on this in chapter 14).

Now is the time to heed the "voice from heaven" and flee from the wrath to come (see Hebrews 12:25–26). Religion, with all its rituals and traditions, cannot save anyone. Only a personal relationship with Jesus Christ will enable you to survive the tests and trials that lie ahead!

> And I heard another voice from heaven saying, "Come out of her, my people, lest you share in her sins, and lest you receive of her plagues." (Rev. 18:4)

How can we identity that great city Babylon so that we can avoid being in covenant with her? By her previous history. Jesus said, "By their fruits you will know them" (Matt. 7:20). There is only *one* ancient, religious system that fulfills the two primary deeds of which she is accused:

> For by your sorcery *all the nations* were deceived. And in her was found *the blood of prophets and saints,* and of all [the martyrs] who were slain on the earth. (Rev. 18:23–24; italics mine)

Only one, worldwide church existed during the days of Thyatira (1517). Only one apostate religion has ever dominated and deceived all the nations of the world. And there is only one that can be accused of being guilty of "the blood of prophets and saints, and of all who were slain [for His name sake] on the earth." Her identity is without question. Neither will there be a question later, because when the first beast arises, she is going to be an integral part of His kingdom.

Jezebel will be judged and chastened during the great tribulation, and not Jezebel only but the rest of the world with her. But it should be noted that the great tribulation is not the wrath of God (although it is the wrath of Satan—see Revelation 12:12). Later, Jezebel will be completely destroyed by unquenchable fire when God's wrath is poured out upon the earth. (His wrath commences with the last trumpet. At that time, two significant things occur—the saints are caught up in the rapture and the first of seven bowls of God's wrath are poured out upon the earth.)

The Antichrist

In Revelation, John introduces the Antichrist as the second of two beasts who appear in the very last days before Christ returns. He obtains his power and position through subtlety and smooth, deceitful speech, deceiving the people into believing that he is their benefactor and convincing the first beast to turn his power over to him (see Daniel 11:32):

> Then I saw another beast coming up out of the earth, and he had two horns like a lamb and spoke like a dragon. *And he exercises all the authority of the first beast in his presence, and causes the earth and those who dwell in it to worship the first beast, whose deadly wound was healed.* He performs great signs, so that he even makes fire come down from heaven on the earth in the sight of men. And he deceives those who dwell on the earth by those signs which he was granted to do in the sight of the beast, *telling those who dwell on the earth to make an image to the beast who was wounded by the sword and lived.* He was granted power to give breath to the image of the beast, that the image of the beast should both speak and cause as many as would not worship the image of the beast to be killed. (Rev. 13:11–15; italics mine)

Those who are deceived by his sorceries are told to make an image of the first beast, from whom he obtained his power. He then gives breath to the image and causes it to speak. We are not told whether this feat is accomplished through sorcery or by modern technology, but advancements in artificial intelligence and other related fields are advancing at an exponential rate. By the time this prophecy is fulfilled, it will probably be technologically possible.

Besides more advancements in technology, there is something else that must transpire before he can appear. In the same way certain conditions had to exists in society before the Protestant Reformation was possible, the world, including the apostate church, must be receptive to the Antichrist's appearing before he can be successful:

> Let no one deceive you by any means; for that Day [the rapture and the commencement of the day of wrath] will not come unless *the falling away comes first,* and the man of sin is revealed, the son of perdition, who opposes and exalts himself above all that is called God or that is worshiped, so that he sits as God *in the temple of God*, showing himself that he is God. Do you not remember that when I was still with you I told you these things? And now you know what is restraining [the doctrine that Jesus is the Messiah], that he [the Antichrist] may be revealed in his own time. For the mystery of lawlessness is already at work; only He who now restrains [Jesus, the true Messiah] will do so until He [His manifest presence] is taken out of the way. (2 Thess. 2:3–7; italics mine)

"He who now restrains will do so until He is taken out of the way." The fact that the church accepts Jesus as their Messiah is what prevents the Antichrist from being able to appear. *Anti* means "in place of." First, before he can take Jesus' place and be accepted as Messiah, the church will have to fall away from the truth, which, as we saw above, is what Paul said would happen:

> Let no one deceive you by any means; for that Day will not come unless the falling away [Greek: *apostasia*, i.e., apostasy] comes first, and the man of sin is revealed, the son of perdition [Greek: *apoleia*, i.e., destroyer]. (2 Thess. 2:3)

Also, there is much debate about the *temple of God* that he sits in, whether it is symbolic of his body or is an actual, physical building. Either one is a future possibility, but at this present time, no one knows whether or not Solomon's temple will be rebuilt in Israel, so we can only wait and see.

Although the Antichrist's motives and deeds are wicked and evil, God allows him to tempt and test the saints to prove whether they love Him with all their heart or not:

> The coming of the lawless one is according to the working of Satan, with all power, signs, and lying wonders, and with all unrighteous deception among those who perish, *because they did not receive the love of the truth*, that they might be saved. And *for this reason God will send them strong delusion, that they should believe the lie*, that they all may be condemned who did not believe the truth but had pleasure in unrighteousness. (2 Thess. 2:9–12; italics mine)

This is a final exam that the saints *must* pass, or they will be eternally lost. Those who fail will not be allowed to graduate and enter into paradise, and there's no second chance:

> Then a third angel followed them, saying with a loud voice, "If anyone worships the beast and his image, and receives his mark on his forehead or on his hand, he himself shall also drink of the wine of the wrath of God, which is poured out full strength into the cup of His indignation. He shall be tormented with fire and brimstone in the presence of the holy angels and in the presence of the Lamb. And the smoke of their torment ascends forever and ever; and they have no rest day or night, who worship the beast and

his image, and whoever receives the mark of his name." (Rev. 14:9–11)

Although immediately before this time, those "who know their God shall be strong, and carry out great exploits" and give powerful witness of the resurrection of Jesus, during the following time of heaven's silence, many will begin to doubt and fall away. Many will believe the Antichrist's lie and accept the beast's mark (see Mark 13:22; Daniel 11:32). Jesus said, "I have come in My Father's name, and you do not receive Me; if another comes in his own name, him you will receive" (John 5:43).

Satan will empower "the son of perdition" to do signs, wonders, and miracles to convince the people that they have been deceived into believing that Jesus actually arose from the dead. *The lie* is that Jesus is a fraud and that the Antichrist is actually the long-awaited messiah. Those who believe this lie and worship the beast and accept his mark will be hopelessly, eternally lost—no exceptions! Beware! So what is his mark? No one knows. but apparently, *it is not 666.* Instead, that is his number. The symbolic meaning of 666 describes his character! (If we knew what his mark will be, it would not be deceptive.)

> He causes all, both small and great, rich and poor, free and slave, to receive a mark on their right hand or on their foreheads, and that no one may buy or sell except one who has the *mark* or the *name* of the beast, or the *number* of his name. Here is wisdom. *Let him who has understanding calculate the number of the beast,* for it is the number of a man: *His number is 666.* (Rev. 13:16–18; italics mine)

In this passage, John appears to give three different ways that one may accept the beast, not just one—his mark, his name, and the number of his name. *His mark and number are not the same thing.* Also, he advises us to use wisdom and "calculate the number of the beast, for it is the number of a man," which is 666. In my book, *The Ultimate Guide to Understanding Your Dreams*, page 67, I have calculated and explained this number, which is a symbolic description of his evil character:

> John identifies the beast as a man. Since we know that this is an evil man, we also know the symbolism used here is negative. Thus, the interpretation is simply this: Six hundred describes a full image, sixty means a rejected image and six simply portrays an image, which John plainly declared is the image of [a carnal] man. So, in the same way that Christ was the express image of the invisible God, this beastly man will be the warped image of the invisible devil. He will fully reflect Satan's despicable image.

The (Broken) Covenant

The Antichrist makes a seven-year covenant "with many," which allows him to peacefully gain power (see Daniel 9:27). Many theologians believe that this covenant is made with Israel, which is possible, but who he actually makes it with is uncertain. Since this covenant affects the whole world, "with many" could mean many nations. Another possibility is this covenant is between the Antichrist, Jezebel, and the first beast's kingdom, since they appear to exist in harmony for the first three and one-half years of the tribulation period. Regardless of who the covenant is with, in the middle of the seven years, he breaks it and executes a takeover of all the world's religions and financial institutions, instituting his own religion and requiring everyone to accept his mark and worship the first beast as their god. As a result, both Jezebel and the saints who remain faithful to Christ and deny his mark are severely persecuted.

The Persecution of the Saints

> Here is the patience of the saints; here are those who keep the commandments of God and the faith of Jesus. Then I heard a voice from heaven saying to me, "Write: 'Blessed are the dead who die in the Lord from now on.'" "Yes," says the Spirit, "that they may rest from their labors, and their works follow them." (Rev. 14:12–13)

The great tribulation will consist of severe persecution of the saints and conclude with nuclear war upon the earth. Although the Antichrist comes in like a lamb, once he obtains control, he quickly reveals his true identity and purpose (see Revelation 13:11).

> He shall speak pompous words against the Most High, Shall persecute the saints of the Most High, And shall intend to change times and law. Then the saints shall be given into his hand for a time and times and half a time. (Dan. 7:25)

Immediately prior to and during this time, Joel's entire prophecy will be fulfilled. (It was only partially fulfilled at Pentecost—see Acts 2:16–21):

> And it shall come to pass afterward that I will pour out My Spirit on all flesh [initially, at Pentecost and then during the end-time, latter-rain ingathering]… And I will show wonders in the heavens and in the earth: Blood and fire and pillars of smoke. The sun shall be turned into darkness, and the moon into blood, before the coming of the great and awesome day of the Lord. And it shall come to pass That whoever calls on the name of the Lord Shall be saved. (Joel 2:28–32)

"Blood, and fire, and pillars [Hebrew: *imara,* erect, as a palm tree, i.e., resembling an atomic mushroom cloud] of smoke" shows that it will be a time of nuclear war. The sun being turned into darkness is symbolic of both God's *grief over making man* and the following time of *heaven's silence,* and the moon being turned into blood shows *severe persecution of the saints.* Jesus' warning concerning the tribulation also confirms that it will be a time of nuclear war:

> For then there will be great tribulation, such as has not been since the beginning of the world until this time, no, nor ever shall be. *And unless those days were shortened, no flesh would be saved*; but for the elect's sake those days will be shortened. (Matt. 24:21–22; italics mine)

Jesus said that if He didn't shorten the duration of the great tribulation, no flesh would be spared. At this present time, nuclear weapons are the only thing capable of annihilating all flesh (all flesh includes men, beasts, fish and birds, not just humanity—see 1 Corinthians 15:39).

Approximately sixty million people were killed by the bubonic plague in the Middle Ages, when a quarter of the world's population was destroyed. During World War Two, over fifty million people were killed in a five-year period, and the infrastructure of many nations was utterly devastated by artillery and aerial bombing. The great tribulation will be far more destructive and disastrous than all the world's plagues, natural calamities, and wars combined. One-third of the world's population, which is a total of almost eight billion people at present, will be slain (over two and one-half billion casualties). We will examine the great tribulation in greater detail in the next chapter.

The Rapture

> Then I looked, and behold, a white cloud, and on the cloud sat One like the Son of Man,

> having on His head a golden crown, and in His hand a sharp sickle. And another angel came out of the temple, crying with a loud voice to Him who sat on the cloud, "Thrust in Your sickle and reap, for the time has come for You to reap, for the harvest of the earth is ripe." So He who sat on the cloud thrust in His sickle on the earth, and the earth was reaped. (Rev. 14:14–16)

There are several different views of the rapture doctrine, including some who say that since the word *rapture* isn't actually in scripture—there isn't one; rather, the rapture is a man-made doctrine without scriptural support. So we need to prove or disprove the rapture doctrine itself before we discuss it any further.

The English word *rapture* is a transliteration of the Greek word *harpazo*, which is translated "caught up" in 1 Thessalonians 4:16–17:

> For the Lord Himself will descend from heaven with a shout, with the voice of an archangel, and with the trumpet of God. And the dead in Christ will rise first. Then we who are alive and remain shall be *caught up* [*harpazo*] together with them in the *clouds* to meet the Lord in the *air*. And thus we shall always be with the Lord. (Italics mine)

Paul said that we would be caught up in the *clouds* (Greek: *nephele*—used twenty-six times and always translated *cloud* or *clouds*), "to meet the Lord in the *air*." The word translated *air* is from the Greek word *aer*, which is used seven times in the New Testament and is always translated by the English word *air*. Therefore, it is clear that Paul expected to be literally "caught up…in the clouds to meet the Lord in the air" when He comes to receive His bride, and we should expect to experience the same thing too.

The first harvest that John saw is a harvest of souls. Jesus said to pray for the Father to send forth laborers into the harvest (see Luke

10:2). Modern-day prophets have prophesied that this end-time harvest is going to add over one billion souls to Christ's kingdom, and James said,

> Therefore be patient, brethren, until the coming of the Lord. See how the farmer waits for the precious fruit of the earth, waiting patiently for it until it receives the early and latter rain. (Jas. 5:7)

Notice that James relates "the coming of the Lord" to the last day harvest. The one is waiting upon the other! Christ won't come back until He has received the full reward for His sacrifice, and as soon as He does, He will return. And when He comes, *it won't be in secret!* The doctrine of a *secret rapture* is a man-made fiction. Although the rapture *is* scriptural, the *secret rapture* is not! It is based upon Jesus saying that no one knows the day nor hour that He is coming because His coming will be as a thief in the night, catching everyone by surprise. The problem is, everyone, saints and sinners alike (figuratively speaking), is going to be home when He arrives! Although they may be surprised by the suddenness of His appearing, and the fact that He comes back when they aren't expecting Him, they certainly won't be unaware of it! There won't be anything secret about it!

> Behold, He is coming with clouds, *and every eye will see Him,* even they who pierced Him. And all the tribes of the earth will mourn because of Him. Even so, Amen. (Rev. 1:7; italics mine)

Another thing, Paul said that the rapture will occur at the "last trump" (see 1 Corinthians 15:52). Announcing something with "a great sound of a trumpet," (as Jesus described it) is certainly not a good way to keep it secret!

> Immediately after the tribulation of those days the sun will be darkened, and the moon will

not give its light; the stars will fall from heaven, and the powers of the heavens will be shaken. *Then the sign of the Son of Man will appear in heaven*, and then all the tribes of the earth will mourn, and *they will see the Son of Man coming* on the clouds of heaven with power and great glory. And He will send His angels *with a great sound of a trumpet,* and they will gather together *His elect* from the four winds, from one end of heaven to the other. (Matt. 24:29–31; italics mine)

Although some theologians teach that *His elect* in the scripture above refers to God gathering the Jews who are dispersed and returning them to Israel, the term "God's elect" also refers to the saints (see Romans 8:33, 11:7; Isaiah 45:4).

As for the doctrine that the church will be raptured before the tribulation so that the saints will not have to overcome the Antichrist and his mark, the following portion of John's second vision distinctly refutes that:

Then I saw an angel coming down from heaven, having the key to the bottomless pit and a great chain in his hand. He laid hold of the dragon, that serpent of old, who is the Devil and Satan, and bound him for a thousand years; and he cast him into the bottomless pit, and shut him up, and set a seal on him, so that he should deceive the nations no more till the thousand years were finished. But after these things he must be released for a little while. And I saw thrones, and they sat on them, and judgment was committed to them. Then I saw the souls of those who had been beheaded for their witness to Jesus and for the word of God, *who had not worshiped the beast or his image, and had not received his mark on their foreheads or on their hands*. And they lived and reigned with Christ for a thousand years. But the rest of the dead did not live again until the thousand years were finished. *This is the first resurrection. Blessed and holy is he who has part in the first resurrection.* Over such the second death has no power, but they shall be priests of God and of Christ, and shall reign with Him a thousand years. (Rev. 20:1–6; italics mine)

It is ludicrous to place the rapture before the mark of the beast because John said that the first resurrection included "those who had been beheaded for their witness to Jesus and for the word of God, *who had not worshiped the beast or his image,* and had not received his mark on their foreheads or on their hands."

It is impossible to be beheaded for refusing to take the mark before it even exists!

The secret rapture doctrine proclaims two resurrections of the just. The first one is a secret rapture that takes place before the tribulation begins, and the second one, which is public, takes place after the tribulation is over. This doctrine fails to take into consideration that John said that the first resurrection included those who refused to take the beast's mark!

If there is a resurrection that takes place before the one that John described, *then the one he described is not the first one!* Jesus said that He is "the Alpha and the Omega, the First and the Last"—and He that is first and last certainly knows what first is! (See Revelation 1:11.) When Jesus came in the flesh, He only mentioned two resurrections of the dead: the resurrection of life and the resurrection of condemnation. Likewise, Paul only mentioned two (see John 5:29; Acts 24:15). In fact, there is absolutely no scripture in the entire Bible that refers to a third rapture or resurrection!

The doctrine of a secret rapture followed by a second one that gives everyone who was unworthy to be in the first one a second chance is *a deadly deception*. This false doctrine will actually help the Antichrist deceive the people. He will be able to claim the church's expectation of the rapture is fraudulent because Jesus still hasn't come, even though the first beast's one-world kingdom and the resultant great tribulation has. He will claim that he is the messiah they've been waiting and looking for and will be able to show supernatural signs and wonders to deceive and convince the people to believe his lies.

It's time for the saints to examine the Scriptures for themselves and prove or disprove the things that they are being taught, especially a doctrine as important as this one. Instead of telling the saints that they should be preparing for the rapture, they should be told to prepare themselves for persecution, because it is already here in many parts of the world, and it will reach every corner of the globe before Jesus returns!

The last scripture about the rapture that we will examine is another one that clearly shows that it takes place after the great tribulation:

> After these things I looked, and behold, *a great multitude which no one could number, of all nations, tribes, peoples, and tongues, standing before the throne and before the Lamb,* clothed with white robes, with palm branches in their hands, and crying out with a loud voice, saying, "Salvation belongs to our God who sits on the throne, and to the Lamb!" All the angels stood around the throne and the elders and the four living creatures, and fell on their faces before the throne and worshiped God, saying: "Amen! Blessing and glory and wisdom, Thanksgiving and honor and power and might, Be to our God forever and ever. Amen." Then one of the elders answered, saying to me, "Who are these arrayed in white robes, and where did they come from?" And I said to him, "Sir, you know." So he said to me, "*These are the ones who come out of the great tribulation, and washed their robes and made them white in the blood of the Lamb.* Therefore they

are before the throne of God, and serve Him day and night in His temple. And He who sits on the throne will dwell among them. They shall neither hunger anymore nor thirst anymore; the sun shall not strike them, nor any heat; for the Lamb who is in the midst of the throne will shepherd them and lead them to living fountains of waters. And God will wipe away every tear from their eyes." (Rev. 7:9–17; italics mine)

In this passage, *John saw a great multitude which no one could number in heaven.* When asked by one of the elders who they were, he confessed his ignorance. Immediately he was told, "These are the ones who come out of the great tribulation"!

With so many scriptures about the rapture and its timing in relation to the tribulation and the mark of the beast, it is difficult to see how the pre-tribulation rapture doctrine ever gained traction in the first place—except that it tickles the ears and sounds a lot more pleasant than "the moon will be turned into blood." Those who have accepted and cling to that delusion are in danger of accepting the next one too, that the man of sin is actually the messiah and that Jesus is a fraud. Jesus said that even some of the very elect would be deceived into accepting the lie. Be wise and arm yourself with the truth! (See Mark 13:22.)

The Great Day of His Wrath

The second harvest that John saw is a harvest of fiery judgment that God has determined to execute upon the ungodly (see Psalm 9:15–16, 11:5–6).

> Then another angel came out of the temple which is in heaven, he also having a sharp sickle. And another angel came out from the altar, who had power over fire, and he cried with a loud cry to him who had the sharp sickle, saying, "Thrust

in your sharp sickle and gather the clusters of the vine of the earth, for her grapes are fully ripe." So the angel thrust his sickle into the earth and gathered the vine of the earth, and threw *it* into the great winepress of the wrath of God. And the winepress was trampled outside the city, and blood came out of the winepress, up to the horses' bridles, for one thousand six hundred furlongs. (Rev. 14:17–20)

Joel also prophesied about this final harvest of God's judgment and the conditions that exist just prior to, and during, its execution:

Proclaim this among the nations: "Prepare for war! Wake up the mighty men, Let all the men of war draw near, Let them come up. Beat your plowshares into swords And your pruning hooks into spears; Let the weak say, 'I am strong.' Assemble and come, all you nations, And gather together all around. Cause Your mighty ones to go down there, O Lord. Let the nations be wakened, and come up to the Valley of Jehoshaphat [Jehovah—judged]; For there I will sit to judge all the surrounding nations. *Put in the sickle, for the harvest is ripe. Come, go down; For the winepress is full, The vats overflow—For their wickedness is great.* Multitudes, multitudes in the valley of decision! For the day of the Lord is near in the valley of decision. The sun and moon will grow dark, And the stars will diminish their brightness. The Lord also will roar from Zion, And utter His voice from Jerusalem; The heavens and earth will shake; But the Lord will be a shelter for His people, And the strength of the children of Israel. So you shall know that I am the Lord your God [when Israel accepts Jesus as their

> Messiah], Dwelling in Zion My holy mountain. *Then Jerusalem shall be holy, And no aliens shall ever pass through her again.*" (Joel 3:9–17; italics mine)

As we continue, we will see that the battle of Armageddon, the battle of Gog and Magog, and Joel's harvest of judgment in the Valley of Jehoshaphat are all prophetic descriptions of the same battle, because each battle ends with the same result—the nation of Israel is once again favored and restored to God.

Thankfully, this is one harvest that we will not be directly involved in except for this one thing—it cannot take place until after we've completed our assignment: to preach the gospel of the kingdom, with the full confirmation of all three witness, to every nation throughout the whole world.

Peter's description of the outpouring of God's wrath affirms that it will resemble a nuclear war:

> But the day of the Lord will come as a thief in the night, in which the heavens will pass away with *a great noise,* and *the elements will melt with fervent heat; both the earth and the works that are in it will be burned up.* Therefore, since all these things will be dissolved, what manner of persons ought you to be in holy conduct and godliness, looking for and hastening the coming of the day of God, *because of which the heavens will be dissolved, being on fire, and the elements will melt with fervent heat?* Nevertheless we, according to His promise, look for new heavens and a new earth in which righteousness dwells. (2 Pet. 3:10–13)

The sequence is this—in the middle of the seven-year tribulation period, the Antichrist institutes his mark, resulting in severe persecution of the saints, followed by the rapture—then the fires of God's wrath are poured out upon the ungodly. Why is the rapture sandwiched in between the great tribulation and God's wrath? Because the church must be lifted up during the fiery purging of the earth in the same way that Noah was lifted up upon the waters while the earth was being purged by the flood. Another similar picture is the angels had to take Lot out of Sodom before God could pour out fire and brimstone upon the city (see Genesis 7:17; 19:22–24).

The actual time between the church being caught up into the clouds to meet the Lord in the air and then returning with Him to rule and reign during the millennium is uncertain, but the number of days between the "sign of the coming of the Son of Man" and the rapture may be as little as forty-five days:

> And from the time that the daily sacrifice is taken away, and the abomination of desolation is set up [which is the sign of the coming of the Son of Man], there shall be one thousand two hundred and ninety days. *Blessed is he who waits*, and comes to the one thousand three hundred and thirty-five days [forty-five days later]. But you, go your way till the end; for you shall rest, and will arise to your inheritance at the end of the days. (Dan. 12:11–13; italics mine)
>
> Looking for *the blessed hope* and glorious appearing [at the rapture] of our great God and Savior Jesus Christ. (Tit. 2:13; italics mine)

The Battle of Armageddon

After the rapture, the church will remain in the air with the Lord until the seven bowls of God's wrath are poured out upon the earth. At the last, seventh bowl, when the Lord descends to fight the battle of Armageddon, we will return to the earth with Him (see Jude 1:14–15):

> Then the seventh angel poured out his bowl into the air, and a loud voice came out of the

temple of heaven, from the throne, saying, "It is done!" (Rev. 16:17)

During this battle, which begins as a concerted effort by all nations to plunder and completely annihilate the nation of Israel, Christ will descend and destroy all the armies of the world. The resulting carnage will surpass anything the world has ever seen (we will examine the battle of Armageddon in greater detail in chapter 13):

> Then I saw an angel standing in the sun; and he cried with a loud voice, saying to all the birds that fly in the midst of heaven, "Come and gather together for the supper of the great God, that you may eat the flesh of kings, the flesh of captains, the flesh of mighty men, the flesh of horses and of those who sit on them, and the flesh of all people, free and slave, both small and great." And I saw the beast, the kings of the earth, and their armies, gathered together to make war against Him who sat on the horse and against His army. Then the beast was captured, and with him the false prophet who worked signs in his presence, by which he deceived those who received the mark of the beast and those who worshiped his image. These two were cast alive into the lake of fire burning with brimstone. And the rest were killed with the sword which proceeded from the mouth of Him who sat on the horse. And all the birds were filled with their flesh. (Rev. 19:17–21)
> And the winepress [of the wrath of God] was trampled outside the city, and blood came out of the winepress, up to the horses' bridles, for one thousand six hundred furlongs [this river of blood will be about two hundred miles long!]. (Rev. 14:20)

The Millennial Kingdom

After the regeneration of all things takes place, the saints will descend back to the earth and rule and reign with Christ for a thousand years (see Revelation 20:4). Some have questioned whether the thousand-year period that John prophesied is literal or symbolic of a longer period of time. Since the millennium corresponds to the seventh day of creation, when God rested, and a day with the Lord is as a thousand years, the thousand years should be considered literal. Both God and the saints enjoy rest (from the unrelenting warfare of this present age) because Satan is imprisoned until the millennium is over.

As for the new heavens and earth that will exist during this time, Peter said, "Nevertheless we, according to His promise, look for new heavens and a new earth in which righteousness dwells" (2 Pet. 3:13). What will this new heaven and earth be like? As for the new heaven, Christ will tabernacle with man:

> None of them shall teach his neighbor, and none his brother, saying, "Know the Lord," for all shall know Me, from the least of them to the greatest of them [and] It shall come to pass That before they call, I will answer; And while they are still speaking, I will hear. (Heb. 8:11; Isa. 65:24)

As for what the new earth will be like, before the flood, all creatures were vegetarians. No one, man or beast, ate meat (see Genesis 1:29–30). The lions ate grass like oxen, and snakes were not poisonous. After the flood, everything changed, and God told Noah, "Every moving thing that lives shall be food for you":

> So God blessed Noah and his sons, and said to them: "Be fruitful and multiply, and fill the earth. And the fear of you and the dread of you shall be on every beast of the earth, on every bird of the air, on all that move on the earth, and on

all the fish of the sea. They are given into your hand. *Every moving thing that lives shall be food for you. I have given you all things, even as the green herbs.* But you shall not eat flesh with its life, that is, its blood." (Gen. 9:1–4; italics mine)

Following the fiery purging process of God's wrath, the earth will be completely regenerated. *There will be a full reset.* Everything will revert to the way it was before the flood, and once again "the lion shall eat straw like the ox":

> The wolf also shall dwell with the lamb, The leopard shall lie down with the young goat, The calf and the young lion and the fatling together; And a little child shall lead them. The cow and the bear shall graze; Their young ones shall lie down together; And the lion shall eat straw like the ox. The nursing child shall play by the cobra's hole, And the weaned child shall put his hand in the viper's den. They shall not hurt nor destroy in all My holy mountain, For the earth shall be full of the knowledge of the Lord As the waters cover the sea. (Isa. 11:6–9)

Not only will the animals peacefully coexist, men will too! Nations "shall beat their swords into plowshares, And their spears into pruning hooks; Nation shall not lift up sword against nation, Neither shall they learn war anymore. But everyone shall sit under his vine and under his fig tree, And no one shall make them afraid" (see Micah 4:3–4). Peace will prevail throughout the whole world until the thousand years are over.

Chapter 12

The Seven Tribulation Trumpets

During the interlude between the sixth and seventh seal (which is where we are at this present time on Revelation's time line of history), the gospel of the kingdom is preached with attesting signs and wonders throughout the earth. Our twofold, end-time task is to gather in the precious fruit of the earth and bring the whole world into accountability (see James 5:7).

Once this final harvest has been gathered in and the third witness has been demonstrated to the whole world, the seventh seal will be opened, releasing the seven tribulation trumpets. The purpose of the great tribulation is twofold—it completes the shaking of both heaven and earth to remove everything that cannot be shaken, which began when the Lamb opened the sixth seal—and in the process, it gives the world one last chance to repent before the wrath to come. (Because of the utter darkness that accompanies the trumpets, it is doubtful that many will be saved during this time, although the door will remain open until the last trumpet blows—see Joel 2:32). The sounding of the last trumpet announces Jesus' return to rapture the church before executing God's fiery wrath upon the ungodly.

The seventh seal consists of seven trumpet blasts, each one releasing calamity upon the earth. Each calamity is more disastrous than the one proceeding it. Although they are certainly horrific, they are not the wrath of God. All the seals, including the seventh, which contains the tribulation trumpets, are redemptive in their purpose, although the seventh seal's purpose includes redeeming the earth from man as well as man from the earth! (See Revelation 11:18.)

The Seventh Seal

> When He opened the seventh seal, *there was silence in heaven for about half an hour*. And I saw the seven angels who stand before God, and to them were given seven trumpets. Then another angel, having a golden censer, came and stood at the altar. He was given much incense, that he should offer it with the prayers of all the saints upon the golden altar which was before the throne. And the smoke of the incense, with the prayers of the saints, ascended before God from the angel's hand. Then the angel took the censer, filled it with fire from the altar, and threw it to the earth. And there were *noises, thunderings, lightnings*, and an *earthquake*. (Rev. 8:1–5; italics mine)

Heaven's half-hour of silence is when the manifestation of Christ's Spirit is withdrawn and the night comes when no man can work. This time of darkness corresponds to the three days of total darkness that Moses afflicted the Egyptians with immediately before the death angel was released upon them (see Exodus 10:21–23). It will last one thousand two hundred and sixty days (see Revelation 12:5–6). During this time the remnant church takes refuge in the wilderness. Jesus said,

> I must work the works of him that sent me, while it is day: the night cometh, when no man

can work. As long as I am in the world, I am the light of the world. (John 9:4–5)

> Behold, the day of the Lord comes, Cruel, with both wrath and fierce anger, To lay the land desolate; And He will destroy its sinners from it. *For the stars of heaven and their constellations Will not give their light; The sun will be darkened in its going forth, And the moon will not cause its light to shine.* (Isa. 13:9–10; italics mine)

Because the world loves darkness rather than light, God cuts off the light. The "stars of heaven" (those saints who have faithfully born witness of Christ's resurrection with great signs and wonders) "will not give their light." Likewise, "The sun will be darkened," and "the moon will not cause its light to shine." The sun represents Christ, and the moon signifies the church. Only those who have built their houses on the Solid Rock will stand during this time of severe testing. After the three and one-half years of total silence is completed, heaven will be vocal once again, although most of the world will be deaf to what it has to say!

The incense mixed with prayer is the combined worship and intercession of millions of saints, who have cried out for justice throughout the centuries but have been denied because up until this point in time, the world could not be held fully accountable (see Deuteronomy 32:4; Luke 18:1–8; Jonah 4:11; Romans 2:4–6). Now their prayers are finally being answered!

Noises (translated *voices* in the KJV, which is more applicable here) represents God speaking in a voice that is understood by the saints. Thunderings, which announce change, are the same voice, but without an interpreter, the world doesn't understand what is being said. When God speaks, worldly people only hear thunder, but God's saints hear and understand His voice (see John 8:43, 10:3–4, 12:28–29). This thunder announces that the harvest of souls is past and judgment has begun. The world is now held fully accountable for its trespasses and sins.

Lightnings represent miraculous demonstrations of God's power, including the administration of His fiery judgments, and, as we've seen before, an earthquake represents God shaking the heavens and the earth to remove that which cannot be shaken. The seventh trumpet adds the symbol of great hail to this list. Hailstones are symbolic of divine judgment being poured out. This introduction of the trumpets shows that although the saints will understand what God is saying and doing during the tribulation, the world will not comprehend what is happening to them.

The mixed blessing of science is that although it has given us much understanding of God's creation, it has blinded and deafened men to the creator Himself! Before the Renaissance, natural calamities as well as bountiful harvests were seen as God's dealings with mankind. Afterward, they were explained by science and accredited to nature. Yet Amos asked, "If a trumpet is blown in a city, will not the people be afraid? If there is calamity in a city, will not the Lord have done it?" (Amos 3:6). God is in full control of nature. It serves Him, as all creation does, with the exception of rebellious mankind!

The Seven Trumpets

The seven trumpet judgments may be summed up in this way: First, a third of all the world's vegetation and one-third of all life in the sea are destroyed. Also, one-third of all the world's fresh water is polluted (possibly by radioactive fallout,) and one-third of the saints are persecuted. Men are severely tormented for five months, and then one-third of all mankind are destroyed in war. At the sounding of the last (seventh) trumpet, the church is raptured, and the seven bowls of God's wrath are poured out upon the earth.

Some theologians teach that the number *one-third* concerning the trumpets is symbolic, but when the fourth seal was opened, *one-fourth* of the world's population was wiped out. During the fourteenth century, the black death and its deadly aftermath (famine, etc.) killed one-fourth of the world's population. Therefore, the trumpets' one-third should also be viewed as literal, although some of the items affected may be symbolic, as the sun, moon, and stars are in the fourth trumpet.

The first trumpet

> So the seven angels who had the seven trumpets prepared themselves to sound. The first angel sounded: And hail and fire followed, mingled with blood, and they were thrown to the earth. And a third of the trees were burned up, and all green grass was burned up. (Rev. 8:6–7)

If God is turning man's sword upon himself (which "hail and fire…mingled with blood" may indicate), this and the following horrific, catastrophic events are probably the results of nuclear war. As we discussed before, nuclear weapons are the only thing that is capable of destroying *all* flesh. Regardless of what causes these calamities, Jesus said that He would shorten the days of the great tribulation; otherwise, no flesh would be spared (see Mark 13:19–20).

On the other hand, if God is using nature to accomplish these chastisements, then perhaps a very large asteroid causes them, especially the first two. Only time will tell. The only thing we can do is wait and see what actually happens, and yes, the church will still be here to witness these events. The rapture does not occur until the last trumpet is sounded.

The second trumpet

> Then the second angel sounded: And something like a great mountain burning with fire was thrown into the sea, and a third of the sea became blood. And a third of the living creatures in the sea died, and a third of the ships were destroyed. (Rev. 8:8–9)

Although these calamities appear sequential, it is possible that they all have a common source and may even occur at the same time. The great mountain burning with fire may represent naval warfare, or if caused by nature, the aforementioned asteroid:

The third trumpet

> Then the third angel sounded: And a great star fell from heaven, burning like a torch, and it fell on a third of the rivers and on the springs of water. The name of the star is Wormwood. A third of the waters became wormwood, and many men died from the water, because it was made bitter. (Rev. 8:10–11)

Some theologians have interpreted this star as a large asteroid. Although asteroids have the potential of being destructive, they don't normally pollute fresh waters and turn them bitter, as this star does. Also, even a large asteroid is local, and this star effects the whole earth. This is something entirely different.

Instead of being the natural waters of the earth, it is entirely possible—and even likely—that the star causing the rivers and the springs of water to become bitter are actually symbolic of a demonic, spiritual deception that imposes a strict caliphate upon a third of the world's population, accompanied with deadly purges of all who resist. (This also agrees with the interpretation of the following fourth trumpet.)

If the star is to be more literally interpreted, then it may be radioactive fallout. The nuclear power plant that had the meltdown in Chernobyl, Ukraine, in 1986, made the world aware of the term *wormwood*, because it was thought that Chernobyl means wormwood in Russian. Wormwood is actually a plant that a bitter, herbal tea is brewed from in that region of the world. Technically, Chernobyl does not mean wormwood, but perhaps the rumor served a good purpose, to make us aware of what could actually happen to our water supply!

The fourth trumpet

> Then the fourth angel sounded: And a third of the sun was struck, a third of the moon, and a third of the stars, so that a third of them were darkened. A third of the day did not shine, and likewise the night. (Rev. 8:12)

This trumpet announces *severe* persecution of the church, which will undoubtedly intensify during the last three and one-half years of the tribulation, as this trumpet depicts. Persecution will increase because the Antichrist will attempt to completely stamp out Christianity from the face of the earth! Although many from the remnant church are hidden in the wilderness during the first three and one-half years of the tribulation period, during the latter half, many will be killed for refusing to take the mark of the beast (see Revelation 12:14–17; Daniel 11:33–35). It appears that the tribulation will be nearly over before the world recognizes the Antichrist for who and what he really is—*the son of perdition*—and by then, it will be too late.

When the forth trumpet sounds, one-third of the saints will be "struck" (imprisoned or killed). Jesus said, "These things I have spoken to you, that in Me you may have peace. In the world you will have tribulation; but be of good cheer, I have overcome the world" (John 16:33). When this time comes, anyone who identifies himself as a Christian will be instantly brought before the authorities. Jesus gives us specific information about the persecution that will transpire immediately after the church completes it commission to reach all nations with the gospel:

> *And the gospel must first be preached to all the nations.* But when they arrest you and deliver you up, do not worry beforehand, or premeditate what you will speak. But whatever is given you in that hour, speak that; for it is not you who speak, but the Holy Spirit. *Now brother will*

> *betray brother to death, and a father his child; and children will rise up against parents and cause them to be put to death.* And you will be hated by all for My name's sake. But he who endures to the end shall be saved. (Mark 13:10–13; italics mine)

This tactic, of turning the people against one another, was used by Hitler to gain control of the German people. Although he had relatively few henchmen to carry out his evil purges, he was able to subject the entire German population to his demonic rule by using a simple method—one that many are now calling *red flag laws!* His method? Authorize and persuade the people to report and accuse anyone they are suspicious of to the authorities—leaving them no place to hide!

After the first four angels blow their trumpets and release their destructive powers upon the world, now there is a shift, and the remaining three pour out destruction directly upon the ungodly people who inhabit the earth (see Revelation 7:1–3).

The three woes:

> And I looked, and I heard an angel flying through the midst of heaven, saying with a loud voice, "*Woe, woe, woe to the inhabitants of the earth*, because of the remaining blasts of the trumpet of the three angels who are about to sound!" (Rev. 8:13; italics mine)

The four preceding trumpet blasts affect sinners and saints alike. The following three brings torment and destruction upon one-third of the world's sinful population. The first of the three (the fifth trumpet) will send a grievous, demonic affliction upon an undisclosed number of men. They will desire to die (repent), but God will not grant them repentance, as Solomon warned:

> Because I have called and you refused, I have stretched out my hand and no one regarded,

> Because you disdained all my counsel, And would have none of my rebuke, I also will laugh at your calamity; I will mock when your terror comes, When your terror comes like a storm, And your destruction comes like a whirlwind, When distress and anguish come upon you. Then they will call on me, but I will not answer; They will seek me diligently, but they will not find me. Because they hated knowledge And did not choose the fear of the Lord, They would have none of my counsel And despised my every rebuke. Therefore they shall eat the fruit of their own way, And be filled to the full with their own fancies. (Prov. 1:24–31)

Those who have mocked God will now be mocked. Those who closed their ears to the gospel and rejected His offer of mercy will now plead for mercy, but it will not be available.

The fifth trumpet

> Then the fifth angel sounded: And I saw a star fallen from heaven to the earth. To him was given the key to the bottomless pit. And he opened the bottomless pit, and smoke [a vast cloud of demons] arose out of the pit like the smoke of a great furnace. So the sun and the air were darkened because of the smoke of the pit. Then out of the smoke locusts came upon the earth. And to them was given power, as the scorpions of the earth have power. *They were commanded not to harm the grass of the earth, or any green thing, or any tree, but only those men who do not have the seal of God on their foreheads.* And they were not given authority to kill them, but to torment them for five months. *Their torment*

was like the torment of a scorpion when it strikes a man. In those days men will seek death and will not find it; they will desire to die, and death will flee from them. The shape of the locusts was like horses prepared for battle. On their heads were crowns of something like gold, and their faces were like the faces of men. They had hair like women's hair, and their teeth were like lions' teeth. And they had breastplates like breastplates of iron, and the sound of their wings was like the sound of chariots with many horses running into battle. They had tails like scorpions, and there were stings in their tails. Their power was to hurt men five months. And they had as king over them the angel of the bottomless pit, whose name in Hebrew is Abaddon, but in Greek he has the name Apollyon. (Rev. 9:1–11; italics mine)

Both Abaddon and Apollyon mean the same thing—*destroyer.* God said that He "created the spoiler to destroy" (Isa. 54:16). During this time, the saints will continue being persecuted, but like the Israelites in Egypt who were exempted from the last seven plagues that afflicted the Egyptians, they will *not* be harmed by this plague. (The locusts were commanded to only harm "those men who do not have the seal of God on their foreheads.") Christians who "are sealed with the Holy Spirit of promise" are exempted (Eph. 1:13; Rev. 3:10). But as we saw above, ungodly men who are tormented by these demonic afflictions will desire to repent, but God will not grant them repentance (see Hebrews 12:16–17).

How do we know that "In those days men will seek death and will not find it; they will desire to die, and death will flee from them" means that even if they repent it will not be accepted? Because unlike the other plagues, where it says, "The rest of mankind, who were not killed by these plagues, did not repent," repentance is not mentioned in this passage (for example, see the sixth trumpet below and Revelation 16:8–11).

Five months after this plague begins, the next trumpet's blast eclipses anything the world has ever seen up to this point in time. It releases nuclear war upon the planet. Knowing this, the five-month time frame gives the saints an opportunity to prepare themselves for what lies ahead (see Mark 13:14–20).

The sixth trumpet

> One woe is past. Behold, still two more woes are coming after these things. Then the sixth angel sounded: And I heard a voice from the four horns of the golden altar which is before God, saying to the sixth angel who had the trumpet, "Release the four angels who are bound at the great river Euphrates." *So the four angels, who had been prepared for the hour and day and month and year, were released to kill a third of mankind.* Now the number of the army of the horsemen was two hundred million; I heard the number of them. And thus I saw the horses in the vision: those who sat on them had breastplates of fiery red, hyacinth blue, and sulfur yellow; and the heads of the horses were like the heads of lions; and out of their mouths came fire, smoke, and brimstone. *By these three plagues a third of mankind was killed*—by the fire and the smoke and the brimstone which came out of their mouths. *For their power is in their mouth and in their tails; for their tails are like serpents, having heads; and with them they do harm.* But the rest of mankind, who were not killed by these plagues, did not repent of the works of their hands, that they should not worship demons, and idols of gold, silver, brass, stone, and wood, which can neither see nor hear nor walk. And they did not repent of their mur-

ders or their sorceries or their sexual immorality or their thefts. (Rev. 9:12–21; italics mine)

As Jeremiah cried out, "O my soul, my soul! I am pained in my very heart! My heart makes a noise in me; I cannot hold my peace, Because you have heard, O my soul, *The sound of the trumpet, The alarm of war*" (Jer. 4:19; italics mine).

Without question, this trumpet unleashes deadly, nuclear war upon the world (the tail, or aftermath, is probably nuclear fallout and radiation poisoning). Although, when this trumpet sounds, there will be a beastly kingdom ruling over all nations on the earth—whether there is any connection or not, no one knows—but at this present time, the only nation capable of raising a two-hundred-million-man army is China. Also, they are presently arming themselves for just such a conflict. John's description of the horses and riders is symbolic of the deadly weapons used by modern armies, such as tanks, assault helicopters, and both conventual and nuclear missiles, issuing fire, smoke, and brimstone—or as it is called today—*shock and awe!*

The Awakening of Israel

Paul said that God blinded Israel and gave her a spirit of slumber, causing them to stumble, "until the fullness of the Gentiles has come in." After the Gentile harvest is over, He will awaken Israel and restore them to Himself (see Romans 11:25).

> Just as it is written: "God has given them a spirit of stupor, Eyes that they should not see And ears that they should not hear, To this very day." And David says: "Let their table become a snare and a trap, A stumbling block and a recompense to them. Let their eyes be darkened, so that they do not see, And bow down their back [in rebellion] always." I say then, have they stumbled that they should fall? Certainly not! But

> through their fall, to provoke them to jealousy, salvation has come to the Gentiles. Now if their fall is riches for the world, and their failure riches for the Gentiles, how much more their fullness! (Rom. 11:8–12)

Concerning their restoration, Paul also said, "For if the casting away of them be the reconciling of the world, what shall the receiving of them be, but life from the dead?" (Rom. 11:15).

At this juncture in Revelation's time line of history, the Gentile harvest is full, so God once again turns His attention to His wayward people, the Israelites. He has never forgotten or withdrawn—nor will He ever forget or withdraw—His promise to Abraham. God made *two* covenants with Abraham—the *gospel* covenant, that in Abraham all families of the earth would be blessed, and the *land* covenant, that his descendants would possess the land of Canaan as an everlasting possession and that He would be their God:

> And I will establish My covenant between Me and you [Abraham] and your descendants after you in their generations, for an everlasting covenant, to be God to you and your descendants after you. Also I give to you and your descendants after you the land in which you are a stranger, all the land of Canaan, as an everlasting possession; and I will be their God. (Gen. 17:7–8)

This covenant was made exclusively with Abraham and his descendants and is separate from the gospel covenant that God made with him in Haran, of which, through the adoption, both the Jew and the Gentiles are partakers:

> Now the Lord had said to Abram: "Get out of your country, From your family And from your father's house, To a land that I will show

you. I will make you a great nation; I will bless you And make your name great; And you shall be a blessing. I will bless those who bless you, And I will curse him who curses you; And in you all the families of the earth shall be blessed." (Gen. 12:1–3; also see Galatians 3:8, 4:5)

The two witnesses:

> Then I was given a reed like a measuring rod. And the angel stood, saying, "Rise and measure the temple of God, the altar, and those who worship there. But leave out the court which is outside the temple, and do not measure it, for it has been given to the Gentiles. And they will tread the holy city underfoot *for forty-two months.* And I will give power to my two witnesses, and they will prophesy one thousand two hundred and sixty days, clothed in sackcloth." These are the two olive trees and the two lampstands standing before the God of the earth. And if anyone wants to harm them, fire proceeds from their mouth and devours their enemies. And if anyone wants to harm them, he must be killed in this manner. These have power to shut heaven, so that no rain falls in the days of their prophecy; and they have power over waters to turn them to blood, and to strike the earth with all plagues, as often as they desire. (Rev. 11:1–6; italics mine)

At this time of world war, God will allow the city of Jerusalem to be overrun for forty-two months. Forty means dominion, and two means to judge. Therefore, God is judging (measuring) Israel and once again bringing them under His rule. During this time, the wayward, sinful Israelites will be afflicted by the two witnesses that appeared with Christ on the Mount of Transfiguration:

> Now it came to pass, about eight days after these sayings, that He took Peter, John, and James and went up on the mountain to pray. As He prayed, the appearance of His face was altered, and His robe became white and glistening. And behold, two men talked with Him, *who were Moses and Elijah.* (Luke 9:28–30; italics mine)

Although many have questioned the identity of the two witnesses, there are several things that aid us in identifying them. The first, and most obvious, is that Moses and Elijah are the ones who appeared with Christ on the Mount of Transfiguration. But the most compelling thing is their ministry itself. Elijah called fire down from heaven, which devoured his enemies, and John said, "Fire proceeds from their mouth and devours their enemies." Elijah also shut heaven, so that it ceased to rain for three and one half years, as the two witness will do—"These have power to shut heaven, so that no rain falls in the days of their prophecy"—which is precisely three and one-half years. Likewise, Moses turned the waters in Egypt to blood and smote the nation with ten plagues, and John said that the two witness "have power over waters to turn them to blood, and to strike the earth with all plagues, as often as they desire."

Although their identity is easily determined, there has also been much debate as to whether they are symbolic, or whether Elijah and Moses will actually come back to minister in person. The Scriptures reveal that *they will return in person.*

There are two different kinds of prophetic writers in Scripture, symbolic and literal. Symbolic writers, such as Daniel in the Old Testament and John in the New, primarily use symbols to portray future events. Prophets like Samuel and Malachi speak plainly. Malachi is a plain-spoken, literal prophetic writer. He said,

> *Behold, I will send you Elijah the prophet Before the coming of the great and dreadful day of the* LORD. And he will turn The hearts of the fathers to the children, And the hearts of the children to their fathers, Lest I come and strike the earth with a curse. (Mal. 4:5–6; italics mine)

Also, when Jesus' disciples asked Him about the return of Elijah, He replied, "Indeed, Elijah is coming first and will restore all things" (Matt. 17:11).

Elijah was caught up in a whirlwind and taken to heaven without dying. Likewise, although Moses died, God sent Michael the archangel to retrieve his body. Why? So that Moses would be able to return "in the flesh" at the appointed time. Jude tells us that Satan, probably knowing in advance God's purpose in retrieving him, had the audacity to oppose Michael:

> Yet Michael the archangel, in contending with the devil, when he disputed about the body of Moses, dared not bring against him a reviling accusation, but said, "The Lord rebuke you!" (Jude 1:9)

There is another indisputable proof that these witness will be two mortal men and not—as some teach—a judgmental anointing exercised by and through certain apostles and prophets of the church. John said that after they are *killed*, people from "tribes, tongues and nations *will see their dead bodies lying in the street* three-and-a-half days" and will rejoice and "send gifts to one another":

> When they finish their testimony, the beast that ascends out of the bottomless pit will make war against them, overcome them, and kill them. And their dead bodies will lie in the street of the great city which spiritually is called Sodom and Egypt, where also our Lord was crucified. *Then*

> *those from the peoples, tribes, tongues, and nations will see their dead bodies three-and-a-half days, and not allow their dead bodies to be put into graves. And those who dwell on the earth will rejoice over them, make merry, and send gifts to one another, because these two prophets tormented those who dwell on the earth.* (Rev. 11:7–10; italics mine)

John is told to "measure the temple of God, the altar, and those who worship there." This measurement (testing or judging) of the temple and the worshippers is specifically directed toward the Jews (see Zechariah 2:1–2). In the same way the purpose of the previous five trumpets is to bring the world to repentance, the ministry of the two witnesses is to bring Israel to repentance (they are clothed in sackcloth, signifying humility and repentance). This is not to say that their ministry will not affect the rest of the world, because the plagues they unleash upon the earth afflict all peoples and nations (see Revelation 11:6, 10).

It is evident from the scriptures quoted above that the Antichrist will kill the two witnesses, but three and a half days later, his evil deed will backfire. The two witnesses are in Israel to preach, with confirming signs, that Jesus is the Messiah, instead of the one who came in his own name whom the world has received. The final confirmation of their testimony concerning the resurrection of Jesus is when God raises them from the dead in the sight of the whole world! (It is interesting to note that at the time of the writing of this prophecy, it wasn't remotely possible for the whole world to watch something like this transpire. The advent of satellite television in 1962 has made this prophecy possible.)

> *Now after the three-and-a-half days the breath of life from God entered them, and they stood on their feet, and great fear fell on those who saw them.* And they heard a loud voice from heaven saying to them, "Come up here." And they ascended to heaven in a cloud, and their enemies saw them.

> In the same hour there was a great earthquake, and a tenth of the city fell. In the earthquake seven thousand people were killed, and the rest were afraid and gave glory to the God of heaven. The second woe is past. Behold, *the third woe is coming quickly.* (Rev. 11:11–14; italics mine)

The seven thunders:

> I saw still another mighty angel coming down from heaven, clothed with a cloud. And a rainbow was on his head, his face was like the sun, and his feet like pillars of fire. He had a little book open in his hand. And he set his right foot on the sea and his left foot on the land, and cried with a loud voice, as when a lion roars. When he cried out, *seven thunders uttered their voices.* Now when the seven thunders uttered their voices, I was about to write; but I heard a voice from heaven saying to me, "*Seal up the things which the seven thunders uttered, and do* not write them." The angel whom I saw standing on the sea and on the land raised up his hand to heaven and swore by Him who lives forever and ever, who created heaven and the things that are in it, the earth and the things that are in it, and the sea and the things that are in it, that there should be delay no longer, *but in the days of the sounding of the seventh angel, when he is about to sound, the mystery of God would be finished*, as He declared to His servants the prophets. (Rev. 10:1–7; italics mine)

Preceding the seventh trumpet, John hears the voice of seven thunders. Although he is forbidden to write what he heard them say, we can glean from the symbols themselves something of value from his experience. First, the angel holding the book has one foot on the earth and one foot on the sea, showing that at this point, God is taking dominion over all the earth (see Joshua 1:3). The number seven means "complete" and thunder means "change," so the voice of the seven thunders are announcing a *complete change* in the world's government! This is confirmed by what the angel said concerning the seventh trumpet; that in the days of the sounding of the seventh trumpet, "there should be delay no longer." The long delay of the coronation of Christ as King over all the earth will finally come to an end. When the seventh trumpet sounds, "The kingdoms of this world…become the kingdoms of our Lord and of His Christ, and He shall reign forever and ever!" (Rev. 11:15).

After hearing the voice of the seven thunders, John was told to go take the little book from the angel who uttered the thunders. The angel gave it to him and told him to eat it, and although it was sweet to his taste, it was bitter to his stomach. We can deduce that the book's contents reveal things that are coming after the sixth trumpet is blown, which is the reason John had to eat it. The angel told him, "You must prophesy again about [the coming rapture of the just and God's fiery judgment upon] many peoples, nations, tongues, and kings" (see Revelation 10:8–11 and Ezekiel 3:2).

God's promises are always sweet to the taste but bitter to the belly. Although all of God's promises are yes and amen, they cannot be obtained without a sacrifice. We follow Jesus' footsteps, and concerning the Father's promises to Him, Hebrews says,

> Looking unto Jesus, the author and finisher of our faith, who for the joy that was set before Him *endured the cross, despising the shame*, and has sat down at the right hand of the throne of God. (Heb. 12:2; italics mine)

In Scripture, each new day begins in the evening, at sundown. Every new revelation, or promise, is like a new day. Invariably, it is quickly followed by the night. Before the morning comes, bringing fulfillment, there is always a time of darkness when our faith is tested. The greater the promise, the greater the struggle and the darker the night. "But recall the former days in which, after you were illuminated, you endured a great struggle with sufferings" (Heb. 10:32).

When Moses went to Egypt and told the children of Israel that God was going to visit them and give them their inheritance, they rejoiced. But before they were able to settle down to live in fulfillment of the promise, they experienced sustained warfare! So it is with every promised inheritance, "The kingdom of heaven suffers violence, and the violent take it by force (Matt. 11:12).

At this juncture, *when the angel is about to sound*, the mystery of godliness has been fully revealed and fulfilled. In fact, as Jesus promised in Mark 4:11, *every mystery* has been revealed to and through the church. The gospel has been fully preached to the whole world, and they have been given all three witnesses. The church has fulfilled its purpose to bear witness of Christ's resurrection through the preaching of the word, the manifestation of the Spirit, and the demonstration of the power of God, so the world is without excuse. Also, the fullness of the Gentile harvest has been brought in, and Israel has been confronted and awakened by the two witnesses concerning their rejection and crucifixion of Jesus the Messiah and their hard-hearted unbelief concerning His resurrection.

God, in His unfathomable love and abundant mercy, has given the world its final opportunity to repent before He pours out his unquenchable fire upon the earth, and many, if not most, have rejected it:

The seventh trumpet

> *Then the seventh angel sounded*: And there were loud voices in heaven, saying, "The kingdoms of this world have become the kingdoms of our Lord and of His Christ, and He shall reign forever and ever!" And the twenty-four elders who sat before God on their thrones fell on their faces and worshiped God, saying: "We give You thanks, O Lord God Almighty, The One who is and who was and who is to come, Because You have taken Your great power and reigned. *The*

nations were angry, and Your wrath has come, And the time of the dead, that they should be judged, And that You should reward Your servants the prophets and the saints, And those who fear Your name, small and great, *And should destroy those who destroy the earth.*" Then the temple of God was opened in heaven, and the ark of His covenant was seen in His temple. And there were lightnings, noises, thunderings, an earthquake, and great hail. (Rev. 11:15–19; italics mine)

One of the signs indicating that we are approaching the very last days is *the nations are angry*, as John said in the passage above. Below is an excerpt from my book, *Practical Christianity* (page 124):

> Why is profane and vulgar language so prevalent in our society today? One reason is profanity-laced speech is often the product of intense anger, and as our national news reports, at this point-in-time the whole world is angry. There's daily reports of everything from street riots to road rage, at home and abroad. The whole world is in a rage! Although few realize it, world-wide-anger and mob violence is a significant indicator of the second coming of Christ.

At the sounding of the seventh trumpet, which Paul referred to as *the last trump*, the long-awaited and longed-for rapture will take place (see 1 Corinthians 15:51–54). At this same time, the first of the seven bowls of God's fiery wrath will be poured out upon the ungodly. God shut the door of Noah's ark so that no one could enter in before the rain started pelting the earth. Likewise, John said, "The temple was filled with smoke from the glory of God and from His power, and no one was able to enter the temple till the seven plagues of the seven angels were completed" (Rev. 15:8). There is absolutely *no second chance* once the tribulation is over and the day of his wrath commences.

Chapter 13

The Seven Bowls of Wrath

> But in the days of the voice of the seventh angel, when he shall begin to sound, the mystery of God should be finished, as he hath declared to his servants the prophets. (Rev. 10:7)

Everything God does is either creative or redemptive of that which He has previously created. Even His wrath is redemptive:

> The nations were angry, and Your wrath has come, And the time of the dead, that they should be judged, And that You should reward Your servants the prophets and the saints, And those who fear Your name, small and great [the rapture], And *should destroy those who destroy the earth*. (Rev. 11:18; italics mine)

The nuclear war, that Jesus cut short during the tribulation, threatened to annihilate all flesh. Now, all the kingdoms of the world that for decades have threatened the world with destruction will be shaken and removed so that only the unshakable kingdom of God may remain.

As Jesus said on the cross, "It is finished." At this point in history, the bride is complete and made herself ready. The church has completed its work. The church age is over, and it's time for the saints to be rewarded for their labors. Every mystery has been revealed, and all things lost have been restored, and every prophecy concerning Christ and the church has been fulfilled.

> And that He may send Jesus Christ, who was preached to you before, whom heaven must receive until the times of restoration of all things, which God has spoken by the mouth of all His holy prophets since the world began. (Acts 3:20–21)
>
> The Lord said to my Lord, "Sit at My right hand, Till I make Your enemies Your footstool." (Ps. 110:1)

Christ's enemies have been made His footstool, and although God isn't through dealing with Israel and the world, as for as the saints are concerned, the war is over, and it is time for them to rest (see Hebrews 4:9–11). It's time for the rapture!

The Rapture

At this juncture, two things happen simultaneously, the rapture and the Day of the Lord commences. How do we know that they both occur at the same time? Because Jesus said that "all tribes of the earth will mourn" when they see Him appear! Likewise, He said that "on the [same] day that Lot went out of Sodom it rained fire and brimstone from heaven and destroyed them all." It will not be a happy time for those who are left behind!

> Immediately after the tribulation of those days the sun will be darkened, and the moon will not give its light; the stars will fall from heaven, and the powers of the heavens will be shaken.

> Then the sign of the Son of Man will appear in heaven, and *then all the tribes of the earth will mourn, and they will see the Son of Man coming on the clouds of heaven with power and great glory. And He will send His angels with a great sound of a trumpet*, and they will gather together His elect from the four winds, from one end of heaven to the other. (Matt. 24:29–31; italics mine)

In the verses above, the stars falling and the powers of heaven being shaken reveal that the Antichrist will continue persecuting the saints right up to the time of the rapture. Also, Jesus cautioned everyone not to be deceived by those who say that you must be in a certain place to be raptured:

> And they will say to you, "Look here!" or "Look there!" *Do not go after them or follow them.* For as the lightning that flashes out of one part under heaven shines to the other part under heaven, so also the Son of Man will be in His day…but *on the day that Lot went out of Sodom it rained fire and brimstone from heaven and destroyed them all. Even so will it be in the day when the Son of Man is revealed.* (Luke 17:23–24, 29–30; italics mine)

The Great Day of the Lord

After the great tribulation is over and the "resurrection of the just" takes place, "the great day of the Lord" is next on God's agenda (see Luke 14:14; Amos 5:18–20). It consists of seven bowls of His wrath being poured out upon the ungodly:

> *The great day of the* Lord *is near*; It is near and hastens quickly. The noise of the day of the Lord is bitter; There the mighty men shall cry

out. *That day is a day of wrath*, A day of trouble and distress, A day of devastation and desolation, A day of darkness and gloominess, A day of clouds and thick darkness. (Zeph. 1:14–15; italics mine)

For the day of the Lord of hosts Shall come upon everything proud and lofty, Upon everything lifted up—And it shall be brought low… The loftiness of man shall be bowed down, And the haughtiness of men shall be brought low; The Lord alone will be exalted in that day, But the idols He shall utterly abolish. They shall go into the holes of the rocks, And into the caves of the earth, From the terror of the Lord And the glory of His majesty, When He arises to shake the earth mightily. (Isa. 2:12, 17–19)

The Seven Bowls of Wrath

Then I saw another sign in heaven, great and marvelous: *seven angels having the seven last plagues, for in them the wrath of God is complete.* And I saw something like a sea of glass mingled with fire, and those who have the victory over the beast, over his image and over his mark and over the number of his name, standing on the sea of glass, having harps of God. They sing the song of Moses, the servant of God, and the song of the Lamb, saying: "Great and marvelous are Your works, Lord God Almighty! Just and true are Your ways, O King of the saints! Who shall not fear You, O Lord, and glorify Your name? For You alone are holy. For all nations shall come and worship before You, *For Your judgments have been manifested*" [though the preceding seven trumpet judgments]. After these things I looked, and behold, the temple of the tabernacle of the testimony in heaven was opened. And out of the temple came the seven angels having the seven plagues, clothed in pure bright linen, and having their chests girded with golden bands. Then one of the four living creatures gave to the seven angels *seven golden bowls full of the wrath of God* who lives forever and ever. The temple was filled with smoke from the glory of God and from His power, and *no one was able to enter the temple till the seven plagues of the seven angels were completed.* (Rev. 15:1–8; italics mine)

At this time, heaven's door is firmly shut. No one is able to enter the temple until the seven plagues are complete. God's righteous judgments have been manifested during the great tribulation, and those who failed to repent and accept God's gracious offer of mercy are now doomed to destruction and eternal damnation. Paul comforted the persecuted Thessalonians with this assurance:

> So that we ourselves boast of you among the churches of God for your patience and faith in all your persecutions and tribulations that you endure, which is manifest evidence of the righteous judgment of God, that you may be counted worthy of the kingdom of God, for which you also suffer; *since it is a righteous thing with God to repay with tribulation those who trouble you,* and to give you who are troubled rest with us *when the Lord Jesus is revealed from heaven with His mighty angels, in flaming fire taking vengeance on those who do not know God, and on those who do not obey the gospel of our Lord Jesus Christ.* These shall be punished with everlasting destruction from the presence of the Lord and from the glory of His power. (2 Thess. 1:4–9; italics mine)

The first bowl

> Then I heard a loud voice from the temple saying to the seven angels, "Go and pour out the bowls of the wrath of God on the earth." So the first went and poured out his bowl upon the earth, and a foul and loathsome sore came upon the men who had the mark of the beast and those who worshiped his image. (Rev. 16:1–2)

Let no man deceive you by any means. God's first act of judgment is to take vengeance upon those who have denied Christ and accepted the Antichrist's lie. Justice will be swift, especially upon those who have participated with him in the persecution of God's people, both Jew and Gentile alike. As we saw when we examined Revelation's time line, the third angel declared that accepting the mark of the beast is an unpardonable sin:

> Then a third angel followed them, saying with a loud voice, "If anyone worships the beast and his image, and receives his mark on his forehead or on his hand, he himself shall also drink of the wine of the wrath of God, which is poured out full strength into the cup of His indignation. He shall be tormented with fire and brimstone in the presence of the holy angels and in the presence of the Lamb. And the smoke of their torment ascends forever and ever; and they have no rest day or night, who worship the beast and his image, and whoever receives the mark of his name." (Rev. 14:9–11)

Take note that *his mark is not 666,* as many think! That is his number! No one knows exactly what his mark will be—so beware; it will be deceptive. (If we knew what it was, it wouldn't be a deception.) Why is accepting the mark of the beast unpardonable? Because accepting his mark signifies that you have rejected and denied that Jesus is your Messiah and have accepted the Antichrist in Christ's place. Jesus said that if you deny Him before men, that He would deny you before the Father (see Matthew 10:33; Hebrews 6:4–6).

The second bowl

> Then the second angel poured out his bowl on the sea, and it became blood as of a dead man; and every living creature in the sea died. (Rev. 16:3)

John's description of God's fiery judgments cannot do justice to the actual terror, turmoil, and destruction these bowls of wrath visit upon the sinners of this world. As we saw from Peter's description of the Lord's wrath, most of the land's buildings and infrastructure—such as airports, seaports, bridges and interstate highways along with houses, planes, trains, ships, cars, trucks, and busses—in addition to almost all human life, are destroyed by fire:

> But the day of the Lord will come as a thief in the night [at a time that they are not expecting it]; in the which the heavens shall pass away with a great noise, and the elements shall melt with fervent heat, the earth also and the works that are therein shall be burned up. (2 Pet. 3:10)

The third bowl

> Then the third angel poured out his bowl on the rivers and springs of water, and they became blood. And I heard the angel of the waters saying: "You are righteous, O Lord, The One who is and who was and who is to be, Because You have judged these things. For they have shed the blood of saints and prophets, And You have given

> them blood to drink. For it is their just due." And I heard another from the altar saying, "Even so, Lord God Almighty, true and righteous are Your judgments." (Rev. 16:4–7)

One modern-day prophet said that God showed him that in the latter days, a barrel of fresh water would be more costly than oil. Although John doesn't mention the source of the blood that is polluting the waters, if it is not supernaturally generated, it is probable that it is coming from the millions and billions of people who are being killed.

The fourth bowl

> Then the fourth angel poured out his bowl on the sun, and power was given to him to scorch men with fire. And men were scorched with great heat, and they blasphemed the name of God who has power over these plagues; and they did not repent and give Him glory. (Rev. 16:8–9)

Here, extreme global warming becomes a reality—not by man's means but by a deliberate act of God—although the massive, explosive power and heat of many hydrogen bombs may have something to do with it. Climatologists tell us that it only takes a tiny shift of the earth's axis to change the entire globe's climate. In a parallel passage, Isaiah said,

> The earth is violently broken, The earth is split open, The earth is shaken exceedingly. The earth shall reel to and fro like a drunkard, And shall totter like a hut; Its transgression shall be heavy upon it, And it will fall, and not rise again. (Isa. 24:19–20)

How can we know that Isaiah's prophecy applies at this time? Because concerning the world, Isaiah said "it will fall, and not rise again." God's wrath will pull down and destroy every kingdom, nation, and city, and they will "not rise again"!

The fifth bowl

> Then the fifth angel poured out his bowl on the throne of the beast, and his kingdom became full of darkness; and they gnawed their tongues because of the pain. They blasphemed the God of heaven because of their pains and their sores, and did not repent of their deeds. (Rev. 16:10–11)

The Antichrist's kingdom, like Hitler's, Stalin's, and Mussolini's before him, who have exalted themselves and ruled using violence and intimidation, will come to an ignoble, contemptible end. There is only one ruler who is worthy to rule the whole world, and that is Jesus, the King of kings and Lord of lords.

The sixth bowl

> Then the sixth angel poured out his bowl on the great river Euphrates, and its water was dried up, so that the way of the kings from the east might be prepared. And I saw three unclean spirits like frogs coming out of the mouth of the dragon, out of the mouth of the beast, and out of the mouth of the false prophet. For they are spirits of demons, performing signs, which go out to the kings of the earth and of the whole world, to gather them to the battle of that great day of God Almighty. "Behold, I am coming as a thief. Blessed is he who watches, and keeps his garments, lest he walk naked and they see his shame." And they gathered them together to

the place called in Hebrew, Armageddon [hill of slaughter]. (Rev. 16:12–16)

At first glance, because Jesus said that He is coming as a thief, this bowl appears to be announcing the return of Christ to rapture the church (which has already taken place at the sounding of the last trump). Instead, it is announcing Christ's unexpected return to the earth with the resurrected saints *when He makes Himself known to His brethren, the Jews.* This warning to watch and "keep his garments" is in reference to those Jews who keep the law but who do not know Jesus as their Messiah. During this battle, many Jews will escape when Christ splits the Mount of Olives with a mighty earthquake, but not everyone who escapes will be accepted as a wedding guest (these are *guests,* not active participants in the wedding itself—see Zechariah 14:3–5; Matthew 22:1–14). This angel sets the earthly stage for the seventh and final bowl to be poured out.

At this juncture, all nations of the world have conspired together and assembled their armies against Jerusalem. (This conspiracy is accomplished through the one-world government that the beast and Antichrist have previously established.) Little do these people know that they are actually being gathered together to be destroyed by the fiery wrath of God.

> And it shall happen in that day that I will make Jerusalem a very heavy stone for all peoples; all who would heave it away will surely be cut in pieces, though all nations of the earth are gathered against it. (Zech. 12:3)

> For I will gather all the nations to battle against Jerusalem; The city shall be taken, The houses rifled, And the women ravished. Half of the city shall go into captivity, But the remnant of the people shall not be cut off from the city. (Zech. 14:2)

The sixth bowl's contents assembles the world's armies to fight their last battle. Once they are assembled, only one bowl is left to finalize the purging of the earth of ungodly, rebellious mankind and usher in the millennial kingdom.

The seventh bowl

Previously, at the sounding of the seventh trumpet, Christ assumed rule over all nations and kingdoms of the world. Now He takes *physical possession* of the kingdoms that are rightfully His:

> Then the seventh angel sounded: And there were loud voices in heaven, saying, "*The kingdoms of this world have become the kingdoms of our Lord and of His Christ*, and He shall reign forever and ever!" (Rev. 11:15; italics mine)

Jesus' obedience to His Heavenly Father, when He came to the world as the Son of man, gave Him the right to claim every Old Testament promise, including dominion over His enemies and the right to rule over all nations (see Deuteronomy 15:6, 28:1, 7; Psalm 2:8–9). Afterward, through His death on the cross, He left everything that He had labored and sacrificed for as an inheritance to all who are adopted into His Heavenly Father's family.

Then, as God instructed Moses in the law, at His resurrection, He became the firstborn of many brethren and received a double portion of that inheritance, of which the rest belongs to all those who are adopted, both Jew and Gentile (see Deuteronomy 21:15–17). Now through His conquest of all kings and kingdoms, He takes full possession of His inheritance, and as the old gospel song so magnificently proclaims, it is time for God to "crown Him Lord of all"!

So when Jesus executes the fierceness of His wrath upon the ungodly, He is exercising the prerogative of kings, executing whomever He wishes and saving alive whomever He wishes (see Daniel 5:14): The sixth bowl set the stage for the final act of the play, and now the battle begins:

> Then the seventh angel poured out his bowl into the air, and a loud voice came out of the temple of heaven, from the throne, saying, "*It is done!*" And there were noises and thunderings and lightnings; and there was a great earthquake, such a mighty and great earthquake as had not occurred since men were on the earth. Now *the great city was divided into three parts*, and the cities of the nations fell. And great Babylon was remembered before God, to give her the cup of the wine of the fierceness of His wrath. Then *every island fled away, and the mountains were not found.* And great hail from heaven fell upon men, *each hailstone about the weight of a talent.* Men blasphemed God because of the plague of the hail, since that plague was exceedingly great. (Rev. 16:17–21; italics mine)

The seventh, and last bowl's contents brings an end to all nations and kingdoms of the world. The thunderings and great earthquake symbolize the final removal of all things that can be shaken, including all the world's governments and religious institutions. The islands and mountains fleeing away show that all the world's nations, both small and great, no longer exist. From this point on, Christ's millennial kingdom, alone, rules over all the earth. The great city being divided depicts the city of Jerusalem's division in the coming battle of Armageddon (where one-third of the Jews are spared). Likewise, during this battle, Mystery Babylon and the Antichrist are completely, utterly destroyed.

This same battle is called the battle of Gog and Magog in Ezekiel, who also mentions the hailstones, but not by weight. Each hailstone weighs about one hundred pounds (at present, the largest hailstones on record weighed about two and one-quarter pounds each):

> "I will call for a sword against Gog throughout all My mountains," says the Lord God.

> "Every man's sword will be against his brother. And I will bring him to judgment with pestilence and bloodshed; I will rain down on him, on his troops, and on the many peoples who are with him, flooding rain, *great hailstones*, fire, and brimstone." (Ezek. 38:21–22; italics mine)

The Battle of Armageddon

When this battle commences, the church is fighting right alongside Christ because once the rapture takes place (which has already occurred at the sound of the last trump), we will forever be with the Lord! John describes this battle again in his second vision, along with the capture and disposal of the beast and false prophet (the Antichrist):

> Then I saw an angel standing in the sun; and he cried with a loud voice, saying to all the birds that fly in the midst of heaven, "Come and gather together for the supper of the great God, that you may eat the flesh of kings, the flesh of captains, the flesh of mighty men, the flesh of horses and of those who sit on them, and the flesh of all people, free and slave, both small and great." And I saw the beast, the kings of the earth, and their armies, gathered together to make war against Him who sat on the horse and against His army. *Then the beast was captured, and with him the false prophet who worked signs in his presence, by which he deceived those who received the mark of the beast and those who worshiped his image. These two were cast alive into the lake of fire burning with brimstone.* And the rest were killed with the sword which proceeded from the mouth of Him who sat on the horse. And all the birds were filled

with their flesh. (Rev. 19:17–21, italics mine; see also Ezekiel 39:17–20)

Jude, quoting an ancient prophecy from the book of Enoch, also describes this battle:

> Now Enoch, the seventh from Adam, prophesied about these men also, saying, "Behold, the Lord comes with ten thousands of His saints, to execute judgment on all, to convict all who are ungodly among them of all their ungodly deeds which they have committed in an ungodly way, and of all the harsh things which ungodly sinners have spoken against Him." (Jude 1:14–15)

It is at this time of extreme fear and anguish that Israel will realize that they have rejected their Messiah and accepted a fraudulent imposter. In that day three, very specific prophecies by Zechariah will be fulfilled:

> And I will pour on the house of David and on the inhabitants of Jerusalem the Spirit of grace and supplication; then they will look on Me whom they pierced. Yes, they will mourn for Him as one mourns for his only son, and grieve for Him as one grieves for a firstborn. (Zech. 12:10)

> And one will say to him, "What are these wounds between your arms?" Then he will answer, "Those with which I was wounded in the house of my friends'... And it shall come to pass in all the land, Says the LORD, That two-thirds in it shall be cut off and die, *But one-third shall be left in it: I will bring the one-third through the fire, Will refine them as silver is refined, And test them as*

gold is tested. They will call on My name, And I will answer them. I will say, "This is My people"; And each one will say, "The Lord is my God." (Zech. 13:6–9; italics mine)

In the passage above, Zechariah declares that when Christ reveals Himself to His brethren, they will finally realize that He is their Messiah. At that time, He will spare one-third of the inhabitants of Israel. They will be surrounded by armies from every nation on earth, and without God's intervention, they are completely without hope:

Then the Lord will go forth And fight against those nations, As He fights in the day of battle. And in that day His feet will stand on the Mount of Olives, Which faces Jerusalem on the east. *And the Mount of Olives shall be split in two, From east to west, Making a very large valley*; Half of the mountain shall move toward the north And half of it toward the south. *Then you shall flee through My mountain valley,* For the mountain valley shall reach to Azal. Yes, you shall flee As you fled from the earthquake In the days of Uzziah king of Judah. *Thus the Lord my God will come, And all the saints with You.* (Zech. 14:3–5; italics mine)

It is during this time of Israel's extreme anguish and affliction that one of Isaiah's most amazing prophecies concerning her will be fulfilled:

Before she was in labor, she gave birth; Before her pain came, She delivered a male child. Who has heard such a thing? Who has seen such things? Shall the earth be made to give birth in one day? *Or shall a nation be born at once?* For as soon as Zion was in labor, She gave birth to her children. (Isa. 66:7–8; italics mine)

As Isaiah said, all Israel will be born (again) in a moment of time! Paul also prophesied of this event:

And so all Israel will be saved, as it is written: "the Deliverer will come out of Zion, And He will turn away ungodliness from Jacob; For this is My covenant with them, When I take away their sins." (Rom. 11:26–27)

This event fulfills the type foreshadowed by the sixth of Israel's seven annual feasts—the Day of Atonement. During this feast, the Israelites must fast and "afflict their souls." The Jews consider this day the holiest day of the year. Once each year, at this festival, the high priest goes into the Holy of Holies and offers the blood of the sacrifice to atone for *all the sins of the whole nation of Israel*, and they are all forgiven, *all at once* (see Leviticus 16:29–34).

Previously, when the first four feasts were fulfilled (Passover through Pentecost), each commenced on the same day the Jews were celebrating that specific feast, so although no one knows what year they will occur, it is probable that both the seven tribulation trumpets and the battle of Armageddon will commence on the actual day that the Jewish feasts are being celebrated, although it is doubtful that they will only occur ten days apart, as the fifth and sixth feasts are. In addition to this, it is also likely that Israel's liberation will take place in the Year of Jubilee. It is not coincidental that the year of Jubilee always starts on the Day of Atonement (see Acts 2:1; Leviticus 23:23–37, 25:8–10).

Why must the Jews "afflict their souls" during the Day of Atonement? Because they are liberated and restored back to God, through Christ, during the battle of Armageddon. Daniel said,

At that time Michael shall stand up, The great prince who stands watch over the sons of

> your people; And there shall be a time of trouble, Such as never was since there was a nation, Even to that time [the great tribulation, followed by the outpouring of God's wrath, ending with the battle of Armageddon]. And at that time your people shall be delivered, Every one who is found written in the book. (Dan. 12:1)

As we mentioned before, the long-awaited battle of Gog and Magog and the battle of Armageddon are one and the same. Armageddon is where it is fought, and Gog (from the land of Magog) is the principal instigator of the battle (see Ezekiel 38:2). It is Christ's intervention for Israel during the battle of Armageddon that causes the Jews to finally come to the realization that Jesus is their Messiah, and Ezekiel says that the battle of Gog and Magog accomplishes the same thing:

> I will set My glory among the nations; all the nations shall see My judgment which I have executed, and My hand which I have laid on them. So the house of Israel shall know that I am the LORD their God from that day forward… And I will not hide My face from them anymore; for I shall have poured out My Spirit on the house of Israel, says the Lord GOD. (Ezek. 39:21–22, 29)

The restoration of Israel back to God is also what Ezekiel's valley of dry bones is depicting (see Ezekiel 37:21–28). Besides prophesying about Israel's recognition and acceptance of Jesus as their Messiah, Zechariah also tells us the horrific and terrifying way that God kills their enemies:

> And this shall be the plague with which the LORD will strike all the people who fought against Jerusalem: Their flesh shall dissolve while they stand on their feet, Their eyes shall dissolve

in their sockets, And their tongues shall dissolve in their mouths. (Zech. 14:12)

Once the earth is purged and its vast population destroyed, there is no longer a nation called America, or China, or England, or any other nation. There is only one kingdom and one King, Jesus the Christ. John said that *every island fled away, and the mountains were not found.* As we previously discussed, islands represent small independent nations, and mountains represent large influential nations and kingdoms. We also saw and discussed the shift of the balance of power, where God was preparing the nations for participation in the battle of Armageddon.

From this point on, the whole earth is the Lord's. There is only one kingdom, the millennial kingdom. Although the continents such as Africa, Europe, and the Americas will still exist, their national boundaries will be redrawn as Christ dictates, according to what He has predestined them to be.

Regardless of what they are called, or what their boundaries are, there is one thing that is certain—the primary seed for their repopulation will be the descendants of Abraham. God will fulfill His irrefutable, immutable promise that He gave Abraham—that Abraham will one day become the father of *many* nations, not just the little nation of Israel!

> As for Me, behold, My covenant is with you, and *you shall be a father of many nations.* No longer shall your name be called Abram, but your name shall be Abraham; *for I have made you a father of many nations.* I will make you exceedingly fruitful; and *I will make nations of you*, and kings shall come from you. And I will establish My covenant between Me and you and your descendants after you in their generations, for an everlasting covenant, to be God to you and your descendants after you. (Gen. 17:4–7; italics mine)

During the battle of Armageddon, one-third of Israel's population will be spared through Christ's intervention when He splits the Mount of Olives and makes a way for them to escape. (At present that would be about 2.5 million Jews.) There are several scriptures that reveal that the Jews who escape and survive will be used during the millennium to repopulate the whole earth, not just the land of Israel. For example, concerning the Jews, Isaiah said,

> For you shall expand to the right and to the left, And your descendants will inherit the nations, And make the desolate cities inhabited… A little one shall become a thousand, And a small one a strong nation. I, the Lord, will hasten it in its time. (Isa. 54:3, 60:22; also see Micah 5:7; Zechariah 10:9–10)

Besides the Jews who escape through the valley created when God splits the Mount of Olives, a few Gentiles will also be spared, but Isaiah said they will be more rare than fine gold (see Isaiah 13:11–13). The severity of God's judgment can be seen by observing what He did in Noah's day. Only eight souls were spared out of an estimated population of 750 million!

Although there will certainly be more than eight spared this time, since the world's current population is 7.8 billion, which is roughly one thousand times more than it was in Noah's day, but how many will be spared remains to be seen. Nevertheless, if the same percentage of the population are destroyed this time as it was then, besides the Jews in Israel who escape, only about eight thousand Gentiles will be spared! Pray that God will remember Habakkuk's prayer and be more lenient this time ("In wrath remember mercy" [see Habakkuk 3:2]).

Those who escape and are spared are *not* immortal. The resurrection has already taken place, and the second one is not until one thousand years later. They are ordinary, mortal people who are spared to reproduce and repopulate the earth during the thousand years of Christ's millennial reign.

Once God's plan for the millennial kingdom is understood, it becomes obvious why Hitler tried to annihilate the entire Jewish population of Europe. Although Hitler obviously didn't know God's intentions, Satan did know and motivated him to build the death camps in a vain attempt to thwart God's plans. Stalin was actually in the process of initiating a similar purge of the Jews in the Soviet Union when he suddenly died—evidently, after the holocaust, God said, "Enough," and mercifully intervened on their behalf. Even today, the angry, anti-Semitic rhetoric and attacks by Iran upon Israel are motivated by Satan's ancient hatred of the Jewish people, who brought forth his nemesis.

Chapter 14

Jezebel and the Antichrist's Judgment

> Then one of the seven angels who had the seven bowls came and talked with me, saying to me, "Come, I will show you the judgment of the great harlot who sits on many waters, with whom the kings of the earth committed fornication, and the inhabitants of the earth were made drunk with the wine of her fornication." (Rev. 17:1–2)

John's second vision begins with an angel showing him "the judgment of the great harlot." Although we've already seen that both Jezebel and the Antichrist are defeated and annihilated in the battle of Armageddon, we will examine their judgment in greater detail here. In the letter to Thyatira, Jesus rebuked the church for allowing "that woman Jezebel, who calls herself a prophetess, to teach and seduce My servants to commit sexual immorality and eat things sacrificed to idols" (Rev. 2:20).

To fully understand the way God sees and describes idolatry, we must realize that adultery and idolatry are essentially the same thing. One is physical and the other spiritual. An adulterer becomes one flesh with an illicit partner, and an idolater becomes one spirit with whatever or whoever he idolizes. Therefore idolatry is literally spiritual adultery.

When Moses led the children of Israel out of Egypt, theologians have always interpreted their departure as symbolic of Christ saving and delivering us from this present, sinful world, but that is only partly correct. Egypt had one of the most advanced religious systems of any nation on earth. They embalmed their dead in preparation for the expected journey in the afterlife and paid homage to many different gods. When Israel left Egypt, some of them carried their Egyptian idols along with them. It wasn't just slavery God delivered them from but rather the religious traditions that they had accepted from the Egyptians from birth. Like many Christians today, they were born into an idolatrous, religious system composed of many meaningless rituals and vain traditions!

God didn't save us to make us religious! Christ died to set us free from religion! God predestined us to be "conformed to the image of his Son," and Paul said that we "were called into the fellowship of His Son, Jesus Christ our Lord" (see Romans 8:29; 1 Corinthians 1:9). We are supposed to walk as Jesus did, free from the rituals and traditions of men. John summed up Christianity in one verse:

> That which we have seen and heard we declare to you, that you also may have fellowship with us; and truly our fellowship is with the Father and with His Son Jesus Christ. (1 John 1:3)

Heaven is not religious, and Christianity should not be, either. Rather than being about religion, as John said, true Christianity is about relationships—first with God, through Christ and the Holy Spirit, and then with one another, through the church. John said, "But if we walk in the light as He is in the light, we have fellowship with one another, and the blood of Jesus Christ His Son cleanses us from all sin" (1 John 1:7).

It is time for God's people to come out of Egypt and abide under the shadow of the Almighty and take refuge under His wings (see Psalm 91:1–4). Jezebel and her adulterous companions are destined to suffer the wrath of God!

Mystery Babylon

> So he carried me away in the Spirit into the wilderness. And I saw a woman sitting on a scarlet beast which was full of names of blasphemy, having seven heads and ten horns. The woman was arrayed in purple and scarlet, and adorned with gold and precious stones and pearls, having in her hand a golden cup full of abominations and the filthiness of her fornication. And on her forehead a name was written: MYSTERY, BABYLON THE GREAT, THE MOTHER OF HARLOTS AND OF THE ABOMINATIONS OF THE EARTH. I saw the woman, drunk with the blood of the saints and with the blood of the martyrs of Jesus. And when I saw her, I marveled with great amazement. But the angel said to me, "Why did you marvel? I will tell you the mystery of the woman and of the beast that carries her, which has the seven heads and the ten horns." (Rev. 17:3–7)

This scriptural passage shows that Babylon is synonymous with Jezebel. One reveals her character (that of a sorceress and a spiritual harlot) and the other of her status as a "city," that is, *an assembly of people sharing common boundaries and subject to common government and laws.* In Scripture, Babylon (alias, Jezebel) is described as a woman and a city. The name Babylon comes from *babel,* which in Hebrew means "confusion."

Ancient Babel was the beginning of Nimrod's kingdom. Nimrod was a "mighty hunter [of souls] before the Lord." In other words, he was a sorcerer—a competitor with God! (See Genesis 10:8–10; Acts

8:9–11, 20:29–30.) His kingdom was the first one-world kingdom recorded in Scripture. God named the capital city Babel, after He destroyed its idolatrous tower, which they were building to enable them to ascend into heaven. He also confused the language of the people and scattered them throughout the earth at the same time (see Genesis 11:1–9).

Babel is the city and kingdom that Nebuchadnezzar rebuilt and exalted to superpower status. Mystery Babylon, where Satan's throne is—who for centuries has competed with God for souls and has attempted to ascend into heaven, to "be like the Most High"—is named after and has the spirit of ancient Babel (see Isaiah 14:12–14; Revelation 2:13). In other words, although the natural kingdom and city fell centuries ago, the spirit of Babel lives on and is operating in and through Mystery Babylon. Therefore, Babel is the kingdom that "was, and is not, and yet is" (now existing in the form of Mystery Babylon, although not yet as a world power, as she was then; see Revelation 17:8).

From this we can see that Mystery Babylon is not simply a church, for it existed long before the church was born. This spirit manifests itself in many labor unions, cults, churches, world religions, and civil governments when their leaders (often unknowingly) practice witchcraft and sorcery. For example, the spirits of witchcraft and sorcery presently manifest themselves in many cults and churches that hold fast to the despised and hated doctrine and deeds of the Nicolaitans, which we discussed previously.

Hitler is a perfect example of a sorcerer. He was under the spell of a Jezebel spirit when he attempted to take over the world and annihilate the Jews. Pharaoh's enslavement and cruel treatment of Israel while they were in Egypt is another prime example:

> The beast that you saw was, and is not, and will ascend out of the bottomless pit and go to perdition. And those who dwell on the earth will marvel, whose names are not written in the Book of Life from the foundation of the world, when they see the beast that was [ancient Babel], and is

not [destroyed and scattered by God in the days of Peleg (see Genesis 10:8–10, 25; 11:1–9)], and yet is [now existing as Mystery Babylon, the harlot religious kingdom]. (Rev. 17:8)

As stated above, Mystery Babylon is more than just a church or religious organization, since it existed before either one of them. The first beast that John saw arise from the sea, for all intents and purposes, is ancient Babel resurrected and thrust upon the world's stage once again as a dominate superpower. It is a kingdom diverse from all others because it arises as a one-world, diplomatic kingdom rather than as a militant kingdom. In some ways, it will be similar to the United Nations. But unlike the United Nations, which has no military or police force of its own, the beast will exercise authority over the combined armies of the world, including their nuclear arsenals and delivery systems. Another more important difference is its reason for existence, which is far more sinister than the peace-keeping function of the United Nations.

Jezebel and this first beast are both motivated by the same spirit and purpose, the power and glory obtained by ruling the whole world (see Matthew 4:8). After AD 313, when Emperor Constantine signed the edict of toleration, ending the persecution of the church, he made Christianity the official religion of the empire and himself head over the church. Afterward, in the process of time, church history reveals that everything reversed and the church became the head of kings and emperors, as the angel explained to John:

> And the woman whom you saw is that great city which reigns over the kings of the earth. (Rev. 17:18).

Beyond any doubt, this next part of John's second vision is the most difficult passage in all of Revelation to interpret:

> Here is the mind which has wisdom: The seven heads are seven mountains [nations or

> kingdoms] on which the woman [Jezebel] sits. There are also seven kings. Five have fallen, one is [Rome], and the other has not yet come [the first beast that rises from the sea]. And when he comes, he must continue a short time [forty-two months]. And the beast that was, and is not, is himself also the eighth, and is of the seven, and is going to perdition [Greek: *apoleia;* ruin or destruction]. (Rev. 17:9–11)

If we allow Scripture to interpret Scripture, as we should, and avoid speculation, then the answer to this riddle should be in the Bible. Daniel lists five world powers for us, although not all by name. They are Babylon, Media, Persia, Greece, and Rome (see Daniel 2:36–40). John said that "five have fallen." If we add ancient Babel, the first world power, to Daniel's list, then we have five that have fallen, leaving Rome, which was still in power at the time John saw his vision.

The eighth kingdom, which is "of the seven," is actually ancient Babel, which was, and is not, and will arise as a world power once again—first as the beast that arises from the sea, who embraces Jezebel and allows her to arise with him, and later as the Antichrist, "the *son* of perdition," who the beast turns his power over to. Therefore, Babel is both the *first* of the five world kingdoms that have fallen, the seventh that has not yet come, and forty-two months after it arises, it morphs into the *eighth* (becoming the Antichrist's kingdom). Therefore, the eighth is "of the seven."

The Mystery of Lawlessness

Paul referred to this demonic trio as "the mystery of lawlessness." The revelation of "the mystery of godliness" is this: God the Father and the Holy Spirit were "manifest in the flesh" through Christ, who is the exact image of the invisible God—conversely, the revelation of "the mystery of lawlessness" will be Satan, the father of lies, and the spirit of witchcraft and sorcery "manifest in the flesh" through the

Antichrist, who will be the exact image of the invisible devil (see 1 Timothy 3:16; Colossians 1:15). Although, before this, Jezebel has been the epitome of sorcery, once the Antichrist comes into power, she is cast down, and he takes her place:

> Let no one deceive you by any means; for that Day will not come unless the falling away comes first, and the man of sin is revealed, the *son* of perdition, who opposes and exalts himself above all that is called God or that is worshiped, so that he sits as God in the temple of God, showing himself that he is God... For *the mystery of lawlessness* is already at work; only He who now restrains will do so until He is taken out of the way. *And then the lawless one will be revealed*, whom the Lord will consume with the breath of His mouth and destroy with the brightness of His coming. The coming of the lawless one is according to the working of Satan, with all power, signs, and lying wonders. (2 Thess. 2:3–4, 7–9; italics mine)

One of the things that make this mystery difficult to unravel is that at first, both Jezebel and the beast that rises from the sea are as one entity. John said that he "saw a woman sitting on a scarlet beast which was full of names of blasphemy, having seven heads and ten horns" (see Revelation 17:3–6). Jezebel sits, or rides, on the beast—signifying that both she and the beast have the same spirit—similar to Jesus riding the white horse in the first seal. The white horse represents the Holy Spirit, and the rider is God in Christ, manifesting Himself to the world through the church. Likewise, the beast has the spirit of Satan, and his rider is Jezebel. So Satan manifests himself to the world through both the beast and his rider, Jezebel, and, a short time later, through the Antichrist.

Jezebel sits as a queen on Satan's throne within the beast's kingdom, and the beast's diplomatic, persuasive power quickly exalts them both to superpower status. This arrangement is similar to that which existed between the Roman emperors and the popes after Constantine made Christianity the state religion. One was political and the other religious, and throughout the centuries, the emperors and popes have been engaged in a constant, unrelenting power struggle for preeminence.

John said this scarlet beast will "make war with the saints and… overcome them" (Rev. 13:7). Since Jezebel rules through the beast's authority, this war may consist of the reinstatement of the deadly inquisitions of the Middle Ages (see 1 Kings 21:5–16). If so, and if she is the primary instigator, it will be short-lived because after only forty-two months, the beast surrenders his position and authority to the Antichrist. It is evident that during this time, Jezebel's wickedness finally reaches the "the fullness of iniquity," bringing God's wrath down upon her without measure (see 1 Thessalonians 2:16; Genesis 15:16; Daniel 8:23).

Once the Antichrist is in power, he releases the ten kings to persecute Jezebel, while he himself heaps his vile wrath upon all those who refuse to worship the first beast and take his mark:

> And the ten horns which you saw on the beast, these will hate the harlot, make her desolate and naked, eat her flesh and burn her with fire. For God has put it into their hearts to fulfill His purpose, to be of one mind, and to give their kingdom to the beast, until the words of God are fulfilled. And the woman whom you saw is that great city which reigns over the kings of the earth. (Rev. 17:16–18)
>
> He who leads into captivity shall go into captivity; he who kills with the sword must be killed with the sword. Here is the patience and the faith of the saints. (Rev. 13:10)

The sea is symbolic of unregenerate, Gentile people and nations. Therefore, the first beast that rises from the sea represents a Gentile kingdom arising in prominence to superpower status. This seven-headed, ten-horned, diplomatic world power does not presently exist (at least not in this form). When it does arise, it only remains in power for forty-two months. Although the emphasis is on the beast as a kingdom, every kingdom has a monarch who rules over it (such as Hitler or Stalin, etc.).

This monarch is the personification of evil, ruling the whole world through diplomatic agreement among nations rather than by force and coercion. John said that God has put it into the hearts of the nations to be of one mind and to willingly surrender their sovereignty to the beast, thus giving him world dominance—but their peaceful coexistence doesn't last long. Paul said,

> For when they say, "Peace and safety!" then sudden destruction comes upon them, as labor pains upon a pregnant woman. And they shall not escape. (1 Thess. 5:3)

Daniel gives us a prophetic picture of the frailty of this coalition of nations in the interpretation of King Nebuchadnezzar's first recorded dream. Verse 44 (below) reveals that the ten-toe portion of this dream is for the latter days, which we are discussing now:

> And the fourth kingdom shall be as strong as iron, inasmuch as iron breaks in pieces and shatters everything; and like iron that crushes, that kingdom will break in pieces and crush all the others [this refers to the Roman empire (27 BC–AD 476). The following, part of this vision refers to the ten kings of the first beast's empire]. Whereas you saw the feet and toes, partly of potter's clay and partly of iron, the kingdom shall be divided; yet the strength of the iron shall be in it, just as you saw the iron mixed with ceramic clay. And as the toes of the feet were partly of iron and partly of clay, so the kingdom shall be partly

strong and partly fragile. As you saw iron mixed with ceramic clay, they will mingle with the seed of men; but they will not adhere to one another, just as iron does not mix with clay. And *in the days of these kings* the God of heaven will set up a kingdom which shall never be destroyed; and the kingdom shall not be left to other people; it shall break in pieces and consume all these kingdoms, and it shall stand forever. (Dan. 2:40–44; italics mine)

The second beast that John saw arises from the earth. The earth is symbolic of man, who is made of the earth's dust. So we see that the first beast isn't just a man but rather a one-world, political kingdom, which becomes a world ruler and persecutes the saints. It will be different (in that the nations will submit willingly), but in some ways, it may be similar to the former Soviet Union, which consisted of fifteen republics and actively persecuted the saints for many years.

This end-time, demonic trinity, consisting of the first beast, Jezebel, and the Antichrist, are all possessed and motivated by the same demons (divination, witchcraft, and sorcery). Therefore, they have identical characteristics and motives—all three seek to dominate and rule the whole world. Likewise, all three hate God and will persecute the saints unmercifully. Because of their similarities, they are almost interchangeable in their roles. Nevertheless, the sequence of their appearing is in this order: Jezebel, who has existed since the time of Nimrod, is like a chameleon. She has used many different disguises and assumed many different roles throughout the centuries, but always for personal gain and glorification. When the first beast arises from the sea, diverse from any kingdom before it, she will be a supporter and collaborator and be an integral part of this kingdom.

This beast will arise as soon as the final harvest of souls is complete. Then, after he has ruled for forty-two months, he will surrender his power and great authority over to the Antichrist. Once the Antichrist is in power, he will turn the ten kings loose against Jezebel, who will persecute her and cast her down (see Revelation 13:11–12, 14:8–9).

The ten kings receive power *one hour* with the beast. The Greek word *hora*, translated "hour" in this verse, can mean a short season (of undetermined length), a day, or an actual hour. Since the monarch they rule with only rules for three and one-half years before turning his power over to the Antichrist, and they continue in power by collaborating with the Antichrist, this one hour is probably about seven years.

As we've already seen in chapter 11, the second beast (who *is* a man) is the Antichrist. He assumes the first beast's authority, thereby becoming a world ruler. The first beast's kingdom still exists during the Antichrist's reign but surrenders its power and authority over to him, symbolized by the two horns that the second beast has ("Then I saw another beast coming up out of the earth, and he had two horns like a lamb and spoke like a dragon" [Rev. 13:1]).

Daniel also saw and wrote about these two beasts. He gives a detailed description of both beasts' rise and fall and their strenuous yet vain attempts to destroy God's people. Because of the detailed and confirming nature of his prophecy, I have inserted explanations within the text and quoted most of it below:

> Daniel spoke, saying, "I saw in my vision by night, and behold, the four winds of heaven were stirring up the Great Sea. And four great beasts came up from the sea, each different from the other. The first was like a lion, and had eagle's wings [Nebuchadnezzar's Babylon]. I watched till its wings were plucked off; and it was lifted up from the earth and made to stand on two feet like a man, and a man's heart was given to it [see Daniel 4:33–37]. And suddenly another beast, a second, like a bear [Medes and Persians]. It was raised up on one side [an unbalanced alliance—Persia was greater than Media], and had three ribs in its mouth between its teeth [an alli-

ance existed between Babylon, Persia, and Media before Babylon was conquered]. And they said thus to it: 'Arise, devour much flesh!' After this I looked, and there was another, like a leopard [Greece], which had on its back four wings of a bird. The beast also had four heads [Alexander the Great's four generals], and dominion was given to it. [the Roman empire arose next, but Daniel skips it and goes directly to the end of days. The following beast is the same one that John saw arise from the sea]. After this I saw in the night visions, and behold, a fourth beast, dreadful and terrible, exceedingly strong. It had huge iron teeth; it was devouring, breaking in pieces, and trampling the residue with its feet. It was different from all the beasts that were before it [obtaining its power though diplomatic agreement, rather than by military takeover], and it had ten horns. I was considering the horns, and there was another horn, a little one, coming up among them, before whom three of the first horns were plucked out by the roots [leaving seven horns]. And there, in this horn, were eyes like the eyes of a man, and a mouth speaking pompous words [the Antichrist]… I watched then because of the sound of the pompous words which the horn was speaking; I watched till the beast was slain, and its body destroyed and given to the burning flame. As for the rest of the beasts, they had their [world] dominion taken away, yet their lives were prolonged for a season and a time [their one world, diplomatic covenant is broken, but they retain their sovereignty as individual nations]. I was watching in the night visions, and behold, One like the Son of Man, coming with the clouds of heaven! [the rapture] He came to the Ancient of Days, and they brought Him near before Him [Christ's second coronation]. Then to Him was given dominion and glory and a kingdom, that all peoples, nations, and languages should serve Him. His dominion is an everlasting dominion, which shall not pass away, and His kingdom is the one which shall not be destroyed... Then I wished to know the truth about the fourth beast [the same as John's first beast that arose from the sea], which was different from all the others, exceedingly dreadful, with its teeth of iron and its nails of bronze, which devoured, broke in pieces, and trampled the residue with its feet; and the ten horns that were on its head, and the other horn which came up, before which three fell, namely, that horn which had eyes and a mouth which spoke pompous words, whose appearance was greater than his fellows [the Antichrist]. I was watching; and the same horn was making war against the saints, and prevailing against them [by instituting the mark of the beast and the persecution that follows], until the Ancient of Days came, and a judgment was made in favor of the saints of the Most High, and the time came for the saints to possess the [millennial] kingdom. Thus he said: 'The fourth beast shall be a fourth kingdom on earth, which shall be different from all other kingdoms, and shall devour the whole earth, trample it and break it in pieces. The ten horns are ten kings who shall arise from [with or of] this kingdom. And another shall rise after them [the Antichrist]; He shall be different from the first ones, and shall subdue three kings. He shall speak pompous words against the Most High, shall persecute the saints of the Most High, and shall intend to change times and law. Then the saints shall be given into his hand for a time and times and half a time [three and one-half years—see Daniel 11:32–35]. But the court shall be seated, and they shall take away his dominion, to consume and destroy it forever. Then the kingdom and dominion, and the greatness of the kingdoms under the whole heaven, shall be given to the people, the saints of the Most High. His kingdom is an everlasting kingdom, and all dominions shall serve and obey Him.'" (Dan. 7:2-8, 11–14, 19–27)

The accuracy of Daniel's prophecy is undeniable. History confirms the rise and fall of the first three kingdoms that he saw—Babylon, the Medes, and Persians—followed by Alexander the Great (who spread Greek culture throughout the known world). Alexander's kingdom was divided among his four generals when he died.

Both the fourth great beast that Daniel saw, that is unlike any that has preceded it, plus the beast representing the Antichrist, have yet to appear. But the technological advances in communication, artificial intelligence, satellite tracking devices, and the move toward implementing a one-world government and digital currency—making it possible to control all personal finances—are speedily paving the way for both the first, one-world, diplomatic kingdom and the Antichrist's debut. Soon, everything will be in place to enable the Antichrist to control all financial transactions, as John said that he will do:

> He causes all, both small and great, rich and poor, free and slave, to receive a mark on their right hand or on their foreheads, and that no one may buy or sell except one who has the mark or the name of the beast, or the number of his name. (Rev. 13:16–17)

Many people (including Martin Luther) have interpreted the Antichrist as a vainglorious pope, which is possible, but there is a strange problem with that view—Mystery Babylon is an ancient religious system that existed long before the first beast arose, whom Jezebel collaborates with as he arises. At some point, the ten kings who are part of that kingdom turn against her and "eat her flesh and burn her with fire"! If she is persecuted by the ten kings, who are part of the beast's kingdom, who has given its power and authority over to the Antichrist, if a pope is the Antichrist, then we have him torturing and killing his own people! Also, at the battle of Armageddon, when God destroys both Jezebel and the Antichrist, they are dealt with separately rather than as one.

It is more probable that the first beast, Jezebel, and, later, the Antichrist will form an alliance, similar to the nonaggression treaty that Hitler and Stalin's made at the beginning of World War Two. Once Hitler thought Germany was strong enough, he broke the treaty and invaded Russia. Likewise, the Antichrist will break the threefold alliance and turn against Jezebel when the opportunity presents itself

Another possibility is the Antichrist is a narcissistic man, similar to an Islamic Imam (Arabic: "leader, model"). The Muslims definitely operate with an Antichrist spirit. At this present time, they are openly persecuting and killing Christians in several different countries. If the Antichrist's father is a Muslim, then his rejection of his father's religion, including rejecting the fictitious reward of seventy virgins, agrees with this interpretation and Daniel's description of him. (If this is correct, instead of glorifying Allah and Muhammad, he will glorify himself and esteem himself as god):

> He shall regard *neither the God of his fathers nor the desire of women,* nor regard any god; for he shall exalt himself above them all. But in their place he shall honor a god of fortresses; and a god which his fathers did not know he shall honor with gold and silver, with precious stones and pleasant things. Thus he shall act against the

> strongest fortresses with a foreign god, which he shall acknowledge, and advance its glory; and he shall cause them to rule over many, and divide the land for gain. (Dan. 11:37–39; italics mine)

Of course, there is always the possibility that he is neither of the above, and that he will invent his own religion, which somewhat agrees with Daniel's description of him. Regardless of who or what the Antichrist is, during this time in history, Jezebel, who has persecuted the saints for centuries, now endures severe persecution herself. The ten kings that arise as part of the first beast's empire will hate her and burn her with fire! (She reaps what she has sown. Her favorite way of torturing and killing those who opposed her was to burn them at the stake.)

> And the ten horns which you saw on the beast, these will hate the harlot, make her desolate and naked, eat her flesh and burn her with fire. (Rev. 17:16)

As we discussed before, Mystery Babylon's fall and destruction will be in two stages. Her first judgment occurs during the great tribulation. During that time, it is likely that Jezebel brazenly competes with the Antichrist for the souls of men. As a result of this vicious power struggle, both Jezebel and those who were enticed and deceived by her sorceries are cast down and severely persecuted, as seen in the following verses of scripture:

> After these things I saw another angel coming down from heaven, having great authority, and the earth was illuminated with his glory. And he cried mightily with a loud voice, saying, "Babylon the great is fallen, is fallen, and has become a dwelling place of demons, a prison for every foul spirit, and a cage for every unclean and hated bird! For all the nations have drunk of the

> wine of the wrath of her fornication, the kings of the earth have committed fornication with her [when she was cast into a sickbed, in fulfillment of Christ's prophecy to her in Revelation 2:20-23], and the merchants of the earth have become rich through the abundance of her luxury." And I heard another voice from heaven saying, "Come out of her, my people, lest you share in her sins, and lest you receive of her plagues. For her sins have reached to heaven, and God has remembered her iniquities. Render to her just as she rendered to you, and repay her double according to her works; in the cup which she has mixed, mix double for her. In the measure that she glorified herself and lived luxuriously, in the same measure give her torment and sorrow; for she says in her heart, 'I sit as queen, and am no widow, and will not see sorrow.'" (Rev. 18:1–7)

After enduring persecution by the ten kings, what is left of her is suddenly and completely destroyed by the fires of God's wrath, during the battle of Armageddon:

> Therefore her plagues will come in one day—death and mourning and famine. And she will be utterly burned with fire, for strong is the Lord God who judges her…"Rejoice over her, O heaven, and you holy apostles and prophets, for God has avenged you on her!" Then a mighty angel took up a stone like a great millstone and threw it into the sea, saying, "Thus with violence the great city Babylon shall be thrown down, and shall not be found anymore… The light of a lamp shall not shine in you anymore, and the voice of bridegroom and bride shall not be heard in you anymore. For your merchants were the great men

of the earth, for by your sorcery all the nations were deceived. And in her was found the blood of prophets and saints, and of all who were slain on the earth." (Rev. 18:8, 20–21, 23–24)

Chapter 15

The Millennial Kingdom

After the great tribulation is over, the rapture takes place, and the bride is caught up in the air to be with the Lord. The actual number of days that the saints will remain in the air with Christ is unknown, but they will return with Him at the battle of Armageddon (see Jude 1:14–15, Revelation 19:14–15).

Either at or immediately after the coronation of Christ as King over all the earth, the marriage supper of the Lamb takes place:

> And I heard, as it were, the voice of a great multitude, as the sound of many waters and as the sound of mighty thunderings, saying, "Alleluia! For the Lord God Omnipotent reigns! Let us be glad and rejoice and give Him glory, for the marriage of the Lamb has come, and His wife has made herself ready." And to her it was granted to be arrayed in fine linen, clean and bright, for the fine linen is the righteous acts of the saints. Then he said to me, "Write: 'Blessed are those who are called to the marriage supper of the Lamb!'" And he said to me, "These are the true sayings of God." (Rev. 19:6–9)

The Feast of Tabernacles

After the marriage supper in heaven and the battle of Armageddon here on earth are over—after the final purging of the earth by the fires of God's wrath is finished—Christ will establish His throne here on the earth, ushering in a thousand-year reign of perfect peace and unprecedented prosperity. At this time, the last of Israel's seven yearly feasts will be fulfilled (the Feast of Tabernacles). During this feast, the Israelites build small booths or "tabernacles" in the fields to live in while gathering in the final harvest of the year. Likewise, Christ will tabernacle with Israel in Jerusalem as the final harvest of flesh-and-blood souls are born and raised here on the earth (see Zechariah 14:16–19).

Those saved before the rapture are considered the *firstfruits* of the main harvest to come. During the millennium, billions will be born, and unlike now, most of them will be saved. Those saved during the millennium will not have the same privileges as the bride of Christ, which is complete at the time of the rapture. Rather, they will be as concubines to the King and servants of the bride. After the millennium is over and the second resurrection takes place, mortal people will no longer exist. Heaven and earth will be as one, and everyone will be immortal.

Ruling with Christ

During the millennium, Christ will rule the earth with a rod of iron. This does not imply harsh, tyrannical rule. Rather, His rule will not be as it is now, only ruling over those who *voluntarily submit,* but He will rule over all mankind, whether they willingly submit or not. The resurrected saints will rule with Him. There *will* be a hierarchy. David will be king over Israel, and each individual tribe will be judged (ruled) by one of the twelve apostles:

> David My servant shall be king over them,
> and they shall all have one shepherd; they shall
> also walk in My judgments and observe My stat-

> utes, and do them. Then they shall dwell in the land that I have given to Jacob My servant, where your fathers dwelt; and they shall dwell there, they, their children, and their children's children, forever; and My servant David shall be their prince forever. Moreover I will make a covenant of peace with them, and it shall be an everlasting covenant with them; I will establish them and multiply them, and *I will set My sanctuary in their midst forevermore. My tabernacle also shall be with them*; indeed I will be their God, and they shall be My people. The nations also will know that I, the LORD, sanctify Israel, when My sanctuary is in their midst forevermore. (Ezek. 37:24–28; italics mine)
>
> So Jesus said to them, "Assuredly I say to you, that in the regeneration, when the Son of Man sits on the throne of His glory, you who have followed Me will also sit on twelve thrones, judging the twelve tribes of Israel." (Matt. 19:28)

As we discussed before, the primary population of the earth will be Abraham's descendants. For a thousand years, the world will be without war, abortion, or disease, so before the thousand years are over, several billion Jews will live on the earth. That is far too many for the land of Israel to contain. In that day, Abraham will truly be the father of many nations.

As an example of what we can expect, in spite of all the Americans killed in wars (totaling over one million men), by abortions (over 62 million babies) and by various diseases, accidents, and murders (untold millions) that America has endured, she has still grown from about 2.5 million in 1776, when she declared her independence, to over 328 million today—a 13,020 percent increase in a span of only 245 years. Even this number is too large for the land of Israel to accommodate, and during the millennium, Abraham's descendants will multiply far more than this!

Our Reward

Regardless of the nationality of the new world's population, every nation, state, and city will be ruled by individuals who were faithful stewards of the gifts that Christ entrusted them with while they were still in this life. Everyone who is worthy to be in the rapture will receive a crown of life (sometimes called a crown of righteousness. Both are referring to being crowned with eternal life—see 2 Timothy 4:8; James 1:12). But there is another crown that isn't gained by inheritance, and that is a crown of glory. These two are not the same. The crown of righteousness is obtained by faith, and the crown of glory is earned by faithful service, suffering, and sacrifice. John said, "Look to yourselves, that we do not lose those things *we worked for*, but that we may receive a full reward" (2 John 1:8; italics mine).

> Therefore [Jesus] said: "A certain nobleman went into a far country to receive for himself a kingdom and to return. So he called ten of his servants, delivered to them ten minas, and said to them, 'Do business till I come'… And so it was that when he returned, having received the kingdom, he then commanded these servants, to whom he had given the money, to be called to him, that he might know how much every man had gained by trading. Then came the first, saying, 'Master, your mina has earned ten minas.' And he said to him, 'Well done, good servant; *because you were faithful in a very little, have authority over ten cities.*' And the second came, saying, 'Master, your mina has earned five minas.' Likewise he said to him, '*You also be over five cities.*'" (Luke 19:12–19; italics mine)

This parable shows that our eternal reward is *proportional* to our service, although Paul said that it isn't *comparable*:

> The Spirit Himself bears witness with our spirit that we are children of God, and if children, then heirs—heirs of God and joint heirs with Christ, if indeed we suffer with Him, that we may also be glorified together. For I consider that the sufferings of this present time are not worthy to be compared with the glory which shall be revealed in us. (Rom. 8:16–18)

Proportional but not comparable! Our service and sufferings are temporary, but our rewards are eternal. Peter said that the crown of glory that Christ rewards us with will never fade away (see 1 Peter 5:1–4).

Besides ruling over cities and nations populated by flesh-and-blood people, we will also be privileged to be their judges. John said, "I saw thrones, and they sat on them, and judgment was committed to them." Paul told the Corinthians that we would judge both men and angels (see 1 Corinthians 6:2–3).

The Garden of Eden

The mortal people who are spared to repopulate the earth also have some wonderful promises to look forward to. Isaiah said they would live as long as a tree!

> For behold, I create new heavens and a new earth; And the former shall not be remembered or come to mind. But be glad and rejoice forever in what I create; For behold, I create Jerusalem as a rejoicing, And her people a joy. I will rejoice in Jerusalem, And joy in My people; The voice of weeping shall no longer be heard in her, Nor the voice of crying. No more shall an infant from there live but a few days, Nor an old man who

has not fulfilled his days; For the child shall die one hundred years old, But the sinner being one hundred years old shall be accursed. They shall build houses and inhabit them; They shall plant vineyards and eat their fruit. They shall not build and another inhabit; They shall not plant and another eat; For as the days of a tree, so shall be the days of My people, And My elect shall long enjoy the work of their hands. (Isa. 65:17–22).

Previously, we saw that during the millennium, everyone and everything, including lions and tigers, all become vegetarians. In Matthew 19:28, when Jesus taught the disciples about the resurrection, He referred to it as "the regeneration." During the millennium, the earth will be regenerated and be as it was in the garden of Eden, before the fall, with the exception that Satan won't be there to tempt anyone. Also, cobras and vipers will no longer be deadly, as they are now:

> The nursing child shall play by the cobra's hole, And the weaned child shall put his hand in the viper's den. They shall not hurt nor destroy in all My holy mountain, For the earth shall be full of the knowledge of the LORD As the waters cover the sea. (Isa. 11:8–9)

It is comforting to know that during the entire thousand years, until the very end, no one will have to contend with the devil. He won't be around to steal, kill, and destroy as he's done since the fall of Adam:

> Then I saw an angel coming down from heaven, having the key to the bottomless pit and a great chain in his hand. He laid hold of the dragon, that serpent of old, who is the Devil and Satan, and bound him for a thousand years; and

he cast him into the bottomless pit, and shut him up, and set a seal on him, so that he should deceive the nations no more till the thousand years were finished. But after these things he must be released for a little while. (Rev. 20:1–3)

Chapter 16

The Great White Throne

The Return of Satan

> Now when the thousand years have expired, Satan will be released from his prison and will go out to deceive the nations which are in the four corners of the earth, Gog and Magog, to gather them together to battle, whose number is as the sand of the sea. They went up on the breadth of the earth and surrounded the camp of the saints and the beloved city. And fire came down from God out of heaven and devoured them. The devil, who deceived them, was cast into the lake of fire and brimstone where the beast and the false prophet are. And they will be tormented day and night forever and ever. (Rev. 20:7–10)

For a reason that is not given, Satan is allowed out of prison and released to go forth and tempt the people to revolt. In the beginning, he led a revolt in heaven, where he tempted many of the angels to rebel against God and follow him. Although tradition says that a third of the angels were cast out with him, as we discussed in chapter 11, that is an error that comes from misinterpreting the symbols used in Revelation 12:4. No one knows the actual number that either side has, but Jesus implied that it is even! Jesus said there are twelve hours in the day, indicating that light and darkness are exactly the same, evenly balanced, with the exception that light always rules over darkness (see John 11:9; Ecclesiastes 2:13).

Jude mentioned what happened to Satan and those who followed him in the beginning, and it has led to another misunderstanding, this one about the source and identity of demons:

> And the angels who did not keep their proper domain, but left their own abode, He has reserved in everlasting chains under darkness for the judgment of the great day. (Jude 1:6)

"Reserved in everlasting chains under darkness" doesn't mean the angels were cast into hell to await their day in court; rather, it refers to their present state of dwelling in darkness rather than in the light of God's countenance. Unlike people, they cannot repent and turn from darkness to light. They are eternally dammed in the same way that someone who blasphemes the Holy Spirit is (see Mark 3:29–29). The devil's angels are demons (see Matthew 25:41). They are free to work here on earth until the judgment of the great and final day (see Matthew 8:29).

God is the creator of all things, both visible and invisible. When He finished His creation, He surveyed all that He had made and said that it was "very good" (Col. 1:16; Gen. 1:31). Therefore, He did not create demons, who are *very bad!* He created angels, who are like you and me. They have a will and are free to follow whoever they choose. Therefore, those who fell made the irreversible decision to follow Satan in his foolish rebellion against God.

This time, instead of angels, Satan leads *people* in a revolt. As before, he fails to obtain his goal, to be equal with God (see Isaiah 14:12–15). He is a loser, and those who are deceived into following him are losers. Apparently, from what John saw, God doesn't waste much time with his wickedness. He puts an end to his rebellion with fire: "And fire came down from God out of heaven and devoured them."

Another thing of interest is John names Gog and Magog in this revolt. Gog, from the land of Magog, is the one who led the world's armies—and was destroyed along with them—when they invaded Israel in the battle of Armageddon (see Ezekiel 38:2). It is evident that Gog, which means to "cover, surmount, or top," isn't actually a man's name but rather a title indicating a *chief prince* or *general*.

THE GREAT WHITE THRONE

The symbolism found in the next part of John's second vision is some of the most fascinating of all:

> Then I saw a great white throne and Him who sat on it, from whose face *the earth and the heaven fled away*. And there was found no place for them. And I saw the dead, small and great, standing before God, and books were opened. And another book was opened, which is the Book of Life. And the dead were judged according to their works, by the things which were written in the books. The *sea* gave up the *dead* who were in it, and *Death* and *Hades* delivered up the dead who were in them. And they were judged, each one according to his works. Then Death and Hades were cast into the *lake of fire*. This is the second death. And anyone not found written in the Book of Life was cast into the lake of fire. (Rev. 20:11–15; italics mine)

At Christ's second coronation, He was made Judge, Lawgiver, and King—not just of the people who willingly submit their lives to Him, as it is now, but of everyone in the entire world (see Isaiah 33:22; Daniel 7:14). So at this time in John's prophecy, the eternal King of all kings sits upon the throne of His glory at the final judgment. "The earth and the heaven fled away," indicating that everything changes from this point on. All things become new. These are *not* to be interpreted literally. As in previous visions, the earth, heaven, and, later, the sea are all symbolic.

Everyone who has ever been born, from the creation of Adam to this point in time—every person who was not in the first resurrection—is now brought before the Judge. Those who are dead are resurrected, and those who are still alive are changed. (Those who were born during the millennium that have not yet died are changed and clothed with immortal bodies, the same as when the rapture took place—see 1 Corinthians 15:50–53.)

"And the books were opened." The books contain the record of all the works of everyone who is standing before the throne. "The sea gave up the dead who were in it, and Death and Hades delivered up the dead who were in them." The *sea* represents all the mortal people on the earth during the millennium, who are still living when this judgment takes place. The *dead* in the sea are those who are not written in the Lamb's book of life. Although they are alive in the flesh, they are spiritually dead in trespasses and sin (see 1 Timothy 5:6).

Death and the grave are synonymous, so *Death* is symbolic of the grave. Death (the grave) delivering up the dead indicates the resurrection of all dead bodies throughout the earth. This includes those who died during the millennium, including both the lost and the saved, plus all those who were lost from the beginning of time. (Those who were lost before the rapture were not included in the first resurrection). *Every* person's dead body, both lost and saved, that was not in the first resurrection, is now resurrected to stand in judgment. *Hades* (hell) indicates those lost souls who died, whose spirits have awaited judgment while they were in hell. They are all given immortal bodies and are brought before Christ's judgment seat (see 1 Peter 3:18–20, 4:6; Luke 16:19–31).

When a saint dies and is buried, his body is in the grave, but his soul and spirit are in heaven with the Lord (see 2 Corinthians 5:8). At the rapture, his soul and spirit are united with his resurrected, immortal body. So it is with the wicked dead; their spirits are in the second hell, and at this (second) resurrection they are each given an immortal body. "For as in Adam all die, even so in Christ all shall be made alive" (1 Cor. 15:22). Both the righteous and the wicked are given an immortal body. A flesh-and-blood body cannot live eternally in heaven nor can it endure the eternal fires of hell. Only an immortal body can (see 1 Corinthians 15:50).

"And the dead were judged according to their works, by the things which were written in the books." Those who thought they were saved but whose faith isn't confirmed by their works are condemned. James said that faith, which isn't confirmed by works, cannot save anyone, because it is dead (see James 2:17, 26):

> Then Death and Hades were cast into the lake of fire. This is the second death. And anyone not found written in the Book of Life was cast into the lake of fire. (Rev. 20:14–15)

In this verse, *death* is symbolic of all the dead bodies that are in the grave, and *hades* (hell) is symbolic of their spirits. At this time, all sinners will experience the second death, which is being cast into the eternal lake of fire. The lake of fire is the third hell. Even as there are three heavens, there are three hells.

The *first hell* is being rejected and separated from God's presence. Conversely, the first heaven is being accepted and dwelling in God's presence. The very day Adam sinned, he died spiritually; that is, he was thrust out of God's presence and fell into the first hell (see Genesis 2:17; 3:22–24). Everyone, from Adam until the end of the millennial kingdom, who chooses to live in sin is dead spiritually and is living in the first hell. This is what happened to Lucifer when he sinned. Because he cannot repent, He is forever barred from paradise (see Isaiah 14:12–15).

The *second hell* is where the soul and spirit of everyone who dies in sin resides (this hell is apparently located somewhere in the lower parts of the earth—see Ephesians 4:9; Psalm 63:9). The *third hell* is the lake of fire. Exactly where it is located, no one knows.

There are three steps and up and three steps down. *All* babies are born innocent. As such, they are born into the first heaven. Their angels commune with their Heavenly Father every day. If a baby is aborted or dies as an infant, he skips the second heaven and goes directly to paradise, into the arms of his loving Heavenly Father (see Mark 10:13–16; Matthew 18:10).

But if a child lives, as he matures, he invariably sins. When he does, his conscience becomes defiled, and he dies spiritually, slipping (unknowingly) into the first hell. If he repents and accepts Christ as his Lord and Savior, he is born again and raised to sit with his Lord in the second heaven. But if he does not repent and dies physically while still in sin, his body goes to the grave, and his soul and spirit descend into the second hell, where he consciously (and regretfully) awaits the final judgment, knowing that he is forevermore damned (see Luke 16:19–27).

Then, at the great white throne, *death* (his body) and *hell* (his soul and spirit) are resurrected and united. Now, as an immortal being, he is judged, condemned, and cast into the eternal lake of fire, which is the third and final fate of those who refuse to repent and submit their lives to Christ.

So to summarize, a person who lives in sin is living in the *first hell*, separated from God. When he dies, his spirit descends into the *second hell*, awaiting the final judgment. Then, at the second resurrection, his body is raised from the grave, and his soul and spirit are taken out of hell and united with his resurrected body. At that time, he is judged and cast into the eternal lake of fire, which is the *third— and lowest—hell*:

The Lowest Hell

> For they are a perverse generation, Children in whom is no faith. They have provoked Me to jealousy by what is not God; They have moved Me to anger by their foolish idols… *For a fire is kindled by my anger, And shall burn to the lowest hell.* (Deut. 32:20–22; italics mine).

For those who are careless about their salvation and have a tendency to flirt with sin, here is a brief, partial description of the lowest hell (see 1 Peter 4:18):

The lake of fire was not originally prepared for man but rather for God's most hated, immortal enemies. As such, it is a place of unimaginable horror. Jesus said that on judgment day, He will say to the lost, "Depart from Me, you cursed, into the everlasting fire prepared for the devil and his angels" (Matt. 25:41).

Everyone who is imprisoned there is immortal—both demons and humans—and each one receives an immutable life sentence. The inmates are completely without hope of ever receiving a reprieve or pardon. And like death that precedes it, there is no escape or discharge from there (see Ecclesiastes 8:8).

Hell's prisoners will be naked and ashamed, yet clothed in total darkness. No light will ever enter there. They will live in excruciating pain caused by searing heat from the eternal flames of an unquenchable fire. They will experience unbearable mental anguish, utter hopelessness coupled with intense grief and loneliness—they will never know the comfort of a loved one or the fellowship of a friend. Every person will have dry mouth and raging, insatiable thirst because there is not a drop of water to be found there. They will weep and wail and grind their teeth from extreme pain and curse the noxious fumes and putrid stench arising from the cauldron of swirling, burning sulfur in which they dwell. Their blasphemous cries, hideous screams, and incessant moans and groans will never cease or abate. They will endure everlasting torment without rest—days without end, years without number—where a thousand years is as a day, and a day is as a thousand years. And above all, their thoughts and lives will be consumed with unimaginable horror as they, with never-ending remorse and deep regret, agonize over how much they lost and how little they gained in exchange for an endless life of torment in the eternal flames of hell (see Jude 1:13; Luke 16:19–31; 2 Peter 2:17; Matthew 25:30; Mark 43–48; Psalm 11:6; Revelation 14:11).

Why would a loving, compassionate God ever choose to send anyone to a place like that? The answer is simple. He does not make that choice—they do. He simply honors the choice they made when they chose darkness over light and spurned His kind and loving offer of mercy and forgiveness.

Although it is often overlooked, there are some who are present in this judgment who are *not* cast into the eternal lake of fire:

> And I saw the dead, small and great, standing before God, and books were opened. And another book was opened, which is the Book of Life. And the dead were judged according to their works, by the things which were written in the books… And anyone not found written in the Book of Life was cast into the lake of fire. (Rev. 20:12, 15)

Those who live during the millennium, whether they were alive or dead at the time of this resurrection, if they are saved, they will receive a reward. Even as those who were in the first resurrection received theirs (see 1 Corinthians 4:5; 2 Corinthians 5:10). Jesus said, "And behold, I am coming quickly, and My reward *is* with Me, to give to every one according to his work" (Rev. 22:12). Amen!

The Bible doesn't actually give us the plan of salvation for the people who live during the millennial reign, but since no one can earn eternal life by their own works, it will probably be as it is now—those who call upon Christ's name and submit their lives to Him in faith will be saved. Those who rebel, such as those who are deceived by Satan at the end, will be eternally dammed.

Chapter 17

The New Jerusalem

> Now I saw a new heaven and a new earth, for the first heaven and the first earth had passed away. Also there was no more sea... Behold, I make all things new. (Rev. 21:1, 5)

All things being made new isn't as we know it in this age. Rather the new heaven and earth will be in a perpetual state of renewal, *never growing old,* even as Paul said that our spirits are now being renewed "day by day" (see 2 Corinthians 4:16; Matthew 6:20). Also, they are not somewhere on a distant planet, but this present heaven and earth will be completely changed by the purging fires of God's wrath and fully restored to its original beauty and bountifulness:

> For this they willfully forget: that by the word of God the heavens were of old, and the earth standing out of water and in the water, by which *the world that then existed* perished, being flooded with water. But *the heavens and the earth which are now* preserved by the same word, are reserved for fire until the day of judgment and perdition of ungodly men. Therefore, since all

> these things will be dissolved, what manner of persons ought you to be in holy conduct and godliness, looking for and hastening the coming of the day of God, because of which the heavens will be dissolved, being on fire, and the elements will melt with fervent heat? Nevertheless we, according to His promise, *look for new heavens and a new earth* in which righteousness dwells. (2 Pet. 3:5–7, 11–13; italics mine)

Likewise, "there was no more sea" doesn't mean that God will dry up the seas. Seas represent mortal, flesh-and-blood people. Mortals will cease to exist after the final regeneration (see 1 Corinthians 15:50). Only immortal people will inhabit the earth. The family of God will be complete.

> Then I, John, saw the holy city, New Jerusalem, coming down out of heaven from God, prepared as a bride adorned for her husband. (Rev. 21:2)

The fact that new Jerusalem is prepared *as* a bride reveals that new Jerusalem *is* the bride! We are the city of God. Although it is difficult for us to envision a city as a living entity, Paul said, "The Jerusalem above is free, which is the mother of us all" (Gal. 4:26).

The church is the body of Christ, God's temple. His Spirit lives in us—not just now as we wait for the resurrection but forever. He has chosen us as the eternal dwelling place of His Spirit! Paul asked, "Do you not know that you are the temple of God and that the Spirit of God dwells in you?" (1 Cor. 3:16).

> And I heard a loud voice from heaven saying, "Behold, the tabernacle of God is with men, and He will dwell with them, and they shall be His people. God Himself will be with them and be their God. And God will wipe away every tear

from their eyes; there shall be no more death, nor sorrow, nor crying. There shall be no more pain, for the former things have passed away." (Rev. 21:3–4)

Everything will be as God originally created it, with one exception—unlike Adam, everyone on earth will be immortal. If animals also inhabit the new earth, they will also be immortal because John said, "There shall be no more death." Although Peter said that God "has given to us all things that pertain to life and godliness," He left out a lot of the details! (See 2 Peter 1:3.) Previously, we saw that during the millennium, lions and bears would peacefully coexist with oxen and lambs, and vipers would be nonpoisonous, but whether these animals will exist as immortal creatures from this point on, no one knows. (Personally, I believe they will, but that's just my opinion, *not* revelation.)

> Then He who sat on the throne said, "Behold, I make all things new." And He said to me, "Write, for these words are true and faithful." And He said to me, "It is done! I am the Alpha and the Omega, the Beginning and the End. I will give of the fountain of the water of life freely to him who thirsts. He who overcomes shall inherit all things, and I will be his God and he shall be My son." (Rev. 21:5–7)

Salvation is available to all. Everyone who thirsts can come and drink from the fountain of the water of life, which is freely given. The pleasures of this life are temporary while the pleasures of heaven are eternal. Only a fool would trade the one for the other. Nevertheless, some fools will!

> But the cowardly, unbelieving, abominable, murderers, sexually immoral, sorcerers, idolaters, and all liars shall have their part in the lake which

burns with fire and brimstone, which is the second death. (Rev. 21:8)

This one verse sums up all sin. The eight sins listed here are actually eight sin categories. Every sin that men commit is found in one or more of these eight categories. Not a single one of them will exist in the third heaven.

Chapter 18

The Lamb's Bride

John's final and shortest vision begins in Revelation 21:9 where he is shown "the great city, the holy Jerusalem, descending out of heaven" and concludes with an invitation for everyone who thirsts to come and drink of the waters of life, followed by a warning for the reader to neither add to nor take away anything from what he has written (Rev. 21:9–22:20). In this vision, an angel shows him Christ's beautiful bride, which, as we discussed in the previous chapter, is a living city, new Jerusalem:

> Then one of the seven angels…came to me and talked with me, saying, "Come, *I will show you the bride, the Lamb's wife.*" And he carried me away in the Spirit to a great and high mountain, and *showed me the great city, the holy Jerusalem*, descending out of heaven from God, having the glory of God. Her light was like a most precious stone, like *a jasper stone* [meaning, he (Christ) will be made prominent], clear as crystal. Also she had a great and high *wall* with *twelve gates*, and twelve angels at the gates, and names written on them, which are the names of the twelve tribes of the children of Israel: three gates on the east,

three gates on the north, three gates on the south, and three gates on the west. Now the wall of the city had *twelve foundations*, and on them were the names of the twelve apostles of the Lamb. (Rev. 21:9–14; italics mine)

As we examine John's vision of the heavenly city, keep in mind that this is a detailed, spiritual description of the perfected church that is presently being constructed:

Now, therefore, you are no longer strangers and foreigners, but fellow citizens with the saints and members of the household of God, *having been built on the foundation of the apostles and prophets, Jesus Christ Himself being the chief corner stone*, in whom the whole building, being joined together, *grows into a holy temple* in the Lord, in whom *you also are being built together for a dwelling place of God* in the Spirit. (Eph. 2:19–22; italics mine)

In the above passage from Revelation, Paul identifies the twelve foundations as the twelve apostles themselves, with Christ as the chief cornerstone (the stone from which all measurements are taken). From this we can deduce that the twelve gates are symbolic of the actual members of the twelve tribes of Israel, who have been redeemed, both before and after the cross. Those who were born before the cross, such as Noah, Abraham, and Moses, believed God and looked forward to the cross, by faith, in the same way that we who are born after the cross look back to it. Salvation is by faith in the sacrificial offering of Christ, alone, both before and after the cross.

And he who talked with me had a gold reed to measure the city, its gates, and its wall. The city is laid out as a square; its length is as great as its breadth. And he measured the city with the reed:

> twelve thousand furlongs. Its length, breadth, and height are equal. Then he measured its wall: one hundred and forty-four cubits, according to the measure of a man, that is, of an angel. The construction of its wall was of jasper; and the city was pure gold, like clear glass. (Rev. 21:15–18)

There are several important things to interpret in this passage. First, *the city is laid out as a square.* In scriptural symbolism, round things are spiritual, and square things are natural or literal. Thus, this city is a literal, physical city, but it isn't like any city that exists on earth today—it is alive! The protective wall of jasper reveals that Christ, who is the wall, *will be made prominent* (see Zechariah 2:4–5), and the city, made of pure, transparent gold, reveals that it exists to glorify God.

Twelve thousand means that the city's citizens are mature saints who are perfectly united in one mind and one accord. The one hundred and forty-four cubits, as we discussed in chapter 9, means full, mature dominion, indicating that these saints have overcome every obstacle Satan could throw at them and have endured unto the end.

John attempted to describe the things that he saw, using language that cannot possibly do justice to them, such as *gold as transparent glass*. Only when we see it for ourselves will we understand, but until then, understand that this city is alive, with living walls, gates, and streets, and everything he is describing is literal, spiritual things being portrayed by natural symbols, as the following verses reveal. This living city is made of "living stones" who have overcome temptation and prevailed:

> If indeed you have tasted that the Lord is gracious. Coming to Him as to a living stone, rejected indeed by men, but chosen by God and precious, you also, as living stones, are being built up a spiritual house, a holy priesthood, to offer up spiritual sacrifices acceptable to God through Jesus Christ. (1 Pet. 2:3–5)

This amazing, eternal city is constructed of faithful, immortal saints, who continually glorify Christ and, with Him, rule the universe!

> The foundations of the wall of the city were adorned with all kinds of precious stones: the first foundation was jasper [he will be made prominent], the second sapphire [telling out], the third chalcedony [copper like; flower like], the fourth emerald [enameled], the fifth sardonyx [ruddy], the sixth sardius [red ones], the seventh chrysolite [gold-stone], the eighth beryl [she will improvise], the ninth topaz [affliction has fled away], the tenth chrysoprase [golden achievement], the eleventh jacinth [hyacinth blue], and the twelfth amethyst [I shall be brought back, (as from a dream)]. (Rev. 21:19–20)

Paul identifies this foundation for us: "For no other foundation can anyone lay than that which is laid, which is Jesus Christ" (1 Cor. 3:11). The mystery of the twelve stones is revealed by what John saw in the latter part of his second vision:

> And I heard a loud voice from heaven saying, "Behold, the tabernacle of God is with men, and He will dwell with them, and they shall be His people. God Himself will be with them and be their God. And God will wipe away every tear from their eyes; there shall be no more death, nor sorrow, nor crying. There shall be no more pain, for the former things have passed away." (Rev. 21:3–4)

Jesus, the One whom God has exalted and *made prominent*, has brought God's creation full circle—from the garden of Eden to the fall, from the fall to the cross, from the cross to the garden—back as one awakening from a horrid, bad dream to a beautiful, glorious sunrise!

> The twelve gates were twelve pearls: each individual gate was of one pearl. And the street of the city was pure gold, like transparent glass. (Rev. 21:21)

The city's walls have twelve gates of pearl, which John identified in verse 12 as the twelve tribes of Israel. Why pearls? Because oysters make pearls by applying a smooth coating over an irritant, and throughout their history, the Jewish people have been hated and persecuted beyond measure yet have endured as a nation and a people in spite of all that Satan has thrown at them. When Christ restores them to the Father, they will once again be honored among all nations.

Why would the twelve tribes be considered *gates*? Because it is *through them* that we have access to all God's precious promises, as Paul said,

> Because to them were committed the oracles of God [and] to whom pertain the adoption, the glory, the covenants, the giving of the law, the service of God, and the promises; of whom are the fathers and from whom, according to the flesh, Christ came, who is over all, the eternally blessed God. Amen. (Rom. 3:2, 9:4–5)

Jesus, the Lamb slain from the foundation of the world, is the light of the world. As the sun never ceases to shine throughout all generations, so Christ, the eternal light, will shine in the full brilliance of His glory forever and forever:

> But I saw no temple in it, for the Lord God Almighty and the Lamb are its temple. The city had no need of the sun or of the moon to shine in

> it, for the glory of God illuminated it. The Lamb is its light.
>
> And the nations of those who are saved shall walk in its light, and the kings of the earth bring their glory and honor into it. Its gates shall not be shut at all by day (there shall be no night there). And they shall bring the glory and the honor of the nations into it. (Rev. 21:22–26)

These kings aren't the kings of this world's present kingdoms but those faithful saints who are crowned with Christ to rule with Him throughout eternity. Paul said, "This is a faithful saying: For if we died with Him, We shall also live with Him. If we endure, We shall also reign with Him." Likewise, Peter promised those ministers who faithfully perform their duties to minister to the saints, "And when the Chief Shepherd appears, you will receive the crown of glory that does not fade away" (2 Tim. 2:11–12; 1 Pet. 5:4).

There will be no rust to tarnish its beauty, nor rot to decay its substance. "But there shall by no means enter it anything that defiles, or causes an abomination or a lie, but only those who are written in the Lamb's Book of Life" (Rev. 21:27).

Chapter 19

The River of Life

> And he showed me a pure river of water of life, clear as crystal, proceeding from the throne of God and of the Lamb. In the middle of its street, and on either side of the river, was the tree of life, which bore twelve fruits, each tree yielding its fruit every month. The leaves of the tree were for the healing of the nations. (Rev. 22:1–2)

Close observation of what John saw reveals that his vision has to be interpreted symbolically, since "the tree of life" is singular and yet he saw "each tree yielding its fruit every month" as though there are twelve trees. In biblical symbolism, a tree is a person (see Isaiah 61:3). The tree that he saw is Christ, who is "the resurrection and the life" (John 11:25). The leaves are His word, as in Psalm 107:20: "He sent His word and healed them, And delivered them from their destructions."

This portion of John's vision corresponds to Ezekiel's vision in 47:1–12, which is similar to John's (especially verse 12). Both Ezekiel's vision and this portion of John's vision appears to apply to the millennium, because healing implies the presence of sickness, and once the millennium is over, there are no mortal people to get sick. Everyone will be immortal. Also, Ezekiel said there were "swamps and marshes" where the river flowed that were not healed (see verse 11).

What actually takes place after the millennium is over and the saints enter into the eternal state, other than the following verses that Paul taught concerning Christ and the resurrection, we know very little:

> But now Christ is risen from the dead, and has become the firstfruits of those who have fallen asleep. For since by man came death, by Man also came the resurrection of the dead. For as in Adam all die, even so in Christ all shall be made alive. But each one in his own order: Christ the firstfruits, afterward those who are Christ's at His coming. Then comes the end, when He delivers the kingdom to God the Father, when He puts an end to all rule and all authority and power. For He must reign till He has put all enemies under His feet. The last enemy that will be destroyed is death [at the great white throne judgment]. For "He has put all things under His feet.' But when He says 'all things are put under Him," it is evident that He who put all things under Him is excepted. Now when all things are made subject to Him, then the Son Himself will also be subject to Him who put all things under Him, that God may be all in all. (1 Cor. 15:20–28)

Although God hasn't provided much insight into this aspect of the future, we do have this assurance in Scripture: "You will show me the path of life; In Your presence is fullness of joy; At Your right hand are pleasures forevermore" (Ps. 16:11).

> And there shall be no more curse, but the throne of God and of the Lamb shall be in it, and His servants shall serve Him. They shall see His face, and His name shall be on their foreheads.

> There shall be no night there: They need no lamp nor light of the sun, for the Lord God gives them light. And they shall reign forever and ever. (Rev. 22:3–5)

Death is abolished. Every curse, including those both in the law and before the law, are vanquished. Everything is restored to its original state, except that the second law of thermodynamics will be suspended. Instead of constant decay, everything will be in a perpetual state of renewal.

In the beginning, God made Eve to help Adam accomplish his assigned task, to dress and keep the garden that was made for them. Likewise, Christ's bride was chosen to serve Him and help Him accomplish whatever the Father assigns Him to do. In this present age, we are assigned the dual task of gathering in the harvest of souls and, through the Holy Spirit, bearing witness to His resurrection. During the millennium, we will judge the world and rule with Him over the nations. Afterward, during the eternal state, we can only imagine what life as the chosen bride of the King of the entire universe will entail.

> Then he said to me, "These words are faithful and true." And the Lord God of the holy prophets sent His angel to show His servants the things which *shortly* take place. "Behold, I am coming *quickly*! Blessed is he who keeps the words of the prophecy of this book." (Rev. 22:6–7; italics mine)

Here, John repeats what he wrote in chapter 1, and as we discussed in that chapter, although his "shortly" and "quickly" doesn't appear very short or quick to us nearly two thousand years later, from God's perspective, those years are merely the blink of an eye:

> Now I, John, saw and heard these things. And when I heard and saw, I fell down to worship

> before the feet of the angel who showed me these things. Then he said to me, "See that you do not do that. For I am your fellow servant, and of your brethren the prophets, and of those who keep the words of this book. Worship God." (Rev. 22:8–9)

This is the second time that John was visited by an immortal messenger who was once a mortal (see Revelation 19:10). This sheds light on what happens when we die and go to be with the Lord—we continue in His service! Jesus said that once those who are saved die physically, "Neither can they die any more: for they are equal unto the angels; and are the children of God, being the children of the resurrection" (Luke 20:36).

> And he said to me, "Do not seal the words of the prophecy of this book, for the time is at hand." (Rev. 22:10)

There has never been a more important time in all of history to understand the mysteries contained in Revelation. There's not much time left. We are now in "the times of restoration of all things, which God has spoken by the mouth of all His holy prophets since the world began" (Acts 3:21). Just as the first four seals that John saw are now history and the contents of the fifth and sixth seal are even now in the process of fulfillment, soon, everything else that he saw will also come to pass. Soon, *not as God sees soon* but as *we see soon*, it will all be over. There's no time to waste!

> He who is unjust, let him be unjust still; he who is filthy, let him be filthy still; he who is righteous, let him be righteous still; he who is holy, let him be holy still. (Rev. 22:11)

It's harvest time. The fields are white and ripe for harvest. Once the earth is reaped, a second, fiery harvest of judgment will commence. It's evening time. Soon the night will come where no man can work. Once the Son goes down, it will be too late. The gospel-ark's ramp will be raised and the door firmly shut.

> And behold, I am coming quickly, and My reward is with Me, to give to every one according to his work... And the Spirit and the bride say, "Come!" And let him who hears say, "Come!" And let him who thirsts come. Whoever desires, let him take the water of life freely... He who testifies to these things says, "Surely I am coming quickly." Amen. Even so, come, Lord Jesus! The grace of our Lord Jesus Christ be with you all. Amen. (Rev. 22:12, 17, 20–21)

Let us close with John's final prayer: "Even so, come, Lord Jesus! The grace of our Lord Jesus Christ be with you all. Amen."

Visitation & Visions	Thunder Changes	Rapture First Resurrection	Wrath of God Fire
V. 1:1–3:22	6:1	7:9–17	6:12–17
V1 4:1–16:21	10:3–4	14:14–16	14:17–20
V2 17:1–21:8	14:2	20:4–6	15:1–16:21
V3 21:9–22:21	16:18		

Seals Book of Life (and Correction)	Churches History	Tribulation Trumpets	Bowls of Wrath 15:6–7
1. 6:1–2	**1.** 2:1–7		
2. 6:3–4	**2.** 2:8–11		
3. 6:5–6	**3.** 2:12–17		
4. 6:7–8	**4.** 2:18–29		
5. 6:9–11	**5.** 3:1–6		
	6. 3:7–13		
	7. 3:14–22		
6. 6:12–17			
7. 8:1–6		**1.** 8:1–7	
		2. 8:8	
		3. 8:10	
		4. 8:12	
		5. 9:1	
		6. 9:13	
		7. 10:7–**11:18**	**1.** 16:1–2
			2. 16:3
			3. 16:4–7
			4. 16:8–9
			5. 16:10–11
			6. 16:12–16
			7. 16:17–21

Second (Last) Resurrection
20:11–15

Bibliography

Baker, Robert A. *A Summary of Christian History.* Broadman & Holman Publishers, 1994

Milligan, Ira. *The Ultimate Guide to Understanding Your Dreams.* Destiny Image, 2012.

———. *The Four Winds.* Servant Ministries, Inc., 2013.

———. *The Church Triumphant.* Servant Ministries, Inc., 2017.

———. *Practical Christianity.* Servant Ministries, Inc., 2022.

Suggested Readings

Ladd, George Eldon. *The Blessed Hope*. William B. Eerdmans Publishing Company, 1956.
Salus, Bill. *Psalm 83*. Prophecy Depot Publishing, 2013.

Other Titles by Ira Milligan

Understanding the Dreams You Dream: Biblical Keys for Hearing God's Voice in the Night

God frequently talks through dreams. The Bible reveals that in the past, dreams were the most common way God talked to His people. Unlike the early Christians, today's believers often treat dreams like junk mail. In doing so, they often throw away the very answers they ask for when they pray for counsel and guidance. *Understanding the Dreams You Dream* is written from a Christian perspective to help Christians understand the symbolic language of dreams. Deliberately written without technical jargon, this book can be easily understood and used by everyone. It is the only complete, one-volume Christian reference book for interpreting dreams on the market today.

The Ultimate Guide to Understanding the Dreams You Dream: Biblical Keys for Hearing God's Voice in the Night

The Ultimate Guide provides insight into your dreams—and your life! Two books in one, it includes a comprehensive dictionary of dream symbols to guide you through the complex world of dreams.

Best-selling author and minister Ira Milligan has decades of personal experience interpreting dreams of his own and those of others. He uses biblical examples to illustrate the way God uses dreams to communicate to His people. This book gives you biblical keys for hearing God's voice in the night through

- specific, detailed directions about hearing God's voice;
- a comprehensive A-Z dictionary of symbol definitions; and

- discerning the difference between dreams God gives and those from other sources. Both normal and abnormal dream situations are presented, enabling you to interpret your own dreams.

The Church Triumphant: Strategies for War

Malachi prophesied that the day was coming when "The Sun of Righteousness shall arise With healing in His wings… You shall trample the wicked, For they shall be ashes under the soles of your feet On the day that I do this, Says the Lord of hosts" (Mal. 4:2–3). Malachi's "You shall trample the wicked, For they shall be ashes under the soles of your feet" exactly parallels Paul's promise, "And the God of peace will crush Satan under your feet shortly" (Rom. 16:20). The church has been waiting and longing for Paul's *shortly* to come to pass now for centuries, and that wonderful day has finally arrived, along with its miraculous healings, abundant provision, and resounding victory—it is an exciting day to be alive! *The Church Triumphant* offers numerous innovative strategies for obtaining victory in this war.

Practical Christianity: Rediscovering the New Testament Church

This book is a field manual for effective spiritual warfare. God's mighty army is disorganized and uncertain of how to fight against the subtle and deceptive hit-and-run tactics the enemy is using. This book's twofold purpose is to provide a biblical training manual to raise up an effective fighting force for war along with detailed instructions for making a new wineskin to serve the new wine that God has for this generation. Our old wineskin cannot contain or sustain the billion soul, end-time harvest that God has planned. To fight and win a billion souls to Christ and then lose them from the lack of a trained workforce to nurture and disciple them would be a catastrophic loss! The time to prepare is now.

The Master's Voice: A Practical Guide to Personal Ministry

    Someone once said, "Experience is the best teacher," and as long as it's someone else's experience, it is! Some things, like ministering the gifts of the Spirit, are *only* learned from personal experience, but it helps to have a few hints along the way. This book is written to share the lessons learned from over thirty years of personal ministry. Both instructional and inspirational, Ira has intermingled a delightful array of scriptural illustrations and personal, real-life experiences to enlighten and inform the reader. Whether you are a seasoned veteran or a complete novice when it comes to operating spiritual gifts, this book is for you. (This book, titled *La Voz del Maestro*, is also available in Spanish.)

Rightly Dividing the Word: Illustrating a Perfect Heart

    One of God's favorite tactics to hide truth is to place it in plain sight but disguise it as something other than what it is. Almost all spiritual truth is first clothed with a natural disguise. When we remove the natural covering, we find the naked truth! Like wheat, the natural husk must be removed from the grain before it is usable. An example of this is Moses's Law. The Law is spiritual, but it is clothed with various commandments and ordinances that hide its precious truths. These spiritual treasures are "life unto those that find them, and health to all their flesh" (Prov. 4:23). *Rightly Dividing the Word* carefully guides the serious Bible student step by step through the scriptures to safely obtain these treasures.

Hidden Mysteries of the Bible: A Foundational Bible Study Course (52 Lessons) Vol. 1

    The Bible is filled with wonderful paradoxes, seeming contradictions, perplexing parables, and intriguing mysteries. One reason for its sometimes difficult but always fascinating makeup is it is composed of two interwoven, parallel journeys that are often confused with one another. One is natural; the other is spiritual. Both contain precious promises, but one is accomplished by merit, the other by grace. This fifty-two-lesson Bible study course guides the student step by step, all the way from the tragic fall of Adam to man's glorious restoration in Christ.

Hidden Mysteries of the Bible: A Foundational Bible Study Course (52 Lessons) Vol. 2

The ability to see into spiritual darkness and positively discern the presence and identity of demons is invaluable. Demons love darkness because they *are* darkness. They are completely repelled by light, and God is light! Effective warfare starts with understanding one's enemy, and spiritual warfare is no exception. Our war with Satan goes beyond our personal battles with him. John said he deceives whole nations. This in-depth Bible course reveals both Satan's tactics and his weaknesses to give God's people a much-needed advantage in their warfare with him.

The Scorpion Within: Illustrating The Wheel of Nature

"Behold, I give unto you power to tread on serpents and scorpions, and over all the power of the enemy" (Luke 10:19). Most Christians know that *serpents* symbolize demons, but very few know the truth and power that lies hidden in the *scorpion's* symbolism. *The Anatomy of a Scorpion* unveils this mystery and reveals its practical application for every believer. A must for anyone interested in counseling and deliverance (this book is accompanied by a separate counselor's aid—the wheel of nature).

Understanding Bible Mysteries: The Truth Shall Make You Free

A wise Christian historian once observed, every major heresy began as a minor deviation from the truth. Heresy is an insidious parasite, thriving by feeding upon the truth. Like counterfeit money, it cannot exist alone. It has to have the substance of truth to survive. Though the consequence of doctrinal error may seem relatively minor in the beginning, the actual harm and damage becomes apparent as it is magnified by time and sustained by tradition.

In Ephesians 4:14, Paul admonished the Saints to "be no more children, tossed to and fro, and carried about with every wind of doctrine," but today's church has been tossed to and fro like a derelict ship on stormy seas. *Understanding Bible Mysteries* calms the winds and straightens the sails to restore balance and stability to the storm tossed ship.

The Hidden Power of Covenant: Releasing the Fullness of the Blessing of the Gospel of Jesus Christ

Paul wrote to the church in Rome and boldly declared, "And I am sure that, when I come unto you, I shall come in the fulness of the blessing of the gospel of Christ" (Rom. 15:29). How could he be so sure? In fact, the New King James Version of the Bible translates Paul as saying, "I *know* that when I come to you, I shall come in the fullness of the blessing." How could he be so confident? What did he know that made him so bold? And besides that, just what *is* the *fulness of the blessing* of the gospel, anyway? The answers are hidden deep in the mystery of covenant. This book probes and explores this mystery to reveal the surprising answers to these important questions.

The Four Winds: Illustrating the Four Winds of Heaven

The Four Winds defines and illustrates the four winds of heaven as they oppose the four winds of the earth (Dan. 7:2; Rev. 7:1). As the story of this ancient conflict unfolds, the role of the prophetic and apostolic ministries in the end-time church is both clarified and explained. The restoration of the prophetic and apostolic ministries is part of God's end-time promise to restore "all things prophesied by the prophets from the beginning of time" (Acts 3:21). *The Four Winds* exposes and defines several changes necessary before this promise can be realized.

Servant Ministries Inc.
Books may be ordered directly from the internet:
www.servant-ministries.org

About the Author

Ira Milligan and his wife, Judy, have served God since 1962. In 1986, they founded Servant Ministries, Inc. They travel internationally and present seminars such as "Dreams and Their Interpretation, Spiritual Warfare, and Prophecy."

www.ingramcontent.com/pod-product-compliance
Lightning Source LLC
LaVergne TN
LVHW010317070526
838199LV00065B/5595